IN THE BEGINNING . . .

Rock crystals are the children of the Earth itself, having formed slowly and laboriously deep beneath the surface of the planet, in much the same manner as a child forms within the womb. They have their origin within the restless, molten magma of the Earth's core.

This mass of molten rock and minerals is accompanied by boiling waters, steam, and gases, which, as they cool, begin to form into crystals, building upon the many minerals deposited within those fissures. In this manner do rock crystals and gemstones begin their development, slowly forming their light in the primeval darkness, taking perhaps 20 to 30 million years to achieve any real size.

Also by Edmund Harold:

VISION TOMORROW

FOCUS ON CRYSTALS

Edmund Harold

**Crystal Illustrations by
Ray Skibinski**

BALLANTINE BOOKS • NEW YORK

First published in 1986 by Greenhouse Publications Pty Ltd, 385 Bridge Road, Richmond, Victoria, Australia

Photography by David Chateris

Illustrations by Ann Becker

ISBN 0-345-34584-3

This edition published by arrangement with Greenhouse Publications

Manufactured in the United States of America

First Ballantine Books Edition: September 1987
Seventh Printing: October 1989

Front cover crystal, courtesy of Richard Berger, Crystal Resources, New York, New York

Foreword

Edmund Harold is a true teacher. His aim is not just to provide people with information about themselves, their bodies, minds and spirits; he also gives them ways in which they can discover it for themselves, and apply it.

At a time of rampant pessimism, when healthy scepticism has been replaced by suspicion, he is prepared to put himself forward and offer instruction in a very deep form of healing. The culture of using crystals goes back for thousands of years. Its emergence now as an authentic means of putting people more in alignment with themselves is hardly surprising when we see a need all around us.

As the world cries out for comfort, it is becoming clear that what is required is spiritual unfoldment, instead of the shrill voice of derision that puts down anything 'supernatural,' and leaves nothing in its place. These opinions, which is all they are, so often are themselves based on superstition. The reality is that science and mysticism are finding a common meeting ground.

Edmund Harold's work is part of a great upsurge of response to people wanting and needing to know themselves better, and take better care of their daily lives. There is a new morning of understanding of the positive use of energy, manifesting itself in many forms, such as the use of color and sound, including chanting, diet, prayer and meditation, as well as other practices such as naturopathy, homeopathy and astrology.

Harold's teachings sit somewhere in the middle of all this. Using quartz crystals as his main tool, he encourages us to monitor ourselves holistically and to become more self reliant. Crystals can be our friends. Coming as they do from the mineral kingdom, they can give us a sense of connection with many levels of life force. His teachings are based on direct knowledge. As he has travelled around the world he has given many workshops. To attend these is to encounter knowledge which seems new, and yet also feels old.

Edmund Harold is no armchair theorist. His teachings are for anybody to explore. He shows us that we are sublime, that we are made up of many parts, that we have not been cast adrift in the universe, that we are part of everything.

Anybody is welcome to make the journey. This book can be a good companion.

John Larkin,
Melbourne,
June, 1986.

 # Contents

Introduction

For more than twenty years I have been deeply involved within the field of natural healing, holding the role of president of a county healing association in Sussex, England, for some nine years. However, I am not a doctor, nor do I hold any medical qualifications.

The suggestions shared herein with regard to the healing of the self are not in any way intended to imply that it can replace established medical treatment, nor should it be used in such a manner. Indeed, I have always taken great pains to emphasise that the swiftest method of returning to full health lies within proper medical treatment, coupled with natural healing. In such a manner both body and spirit are restored to harmony.

All information shared within these pages can be proved by simple experimentation—provided that the person concerned is in any way sensitive to these potent energies.

FOCUS ON
CRYSTALS

◇◇◇◇◇◇◇◇◇◇◇◇◇◇◇◇◇◇◇◇◇◇◇◇◇◇◇◇◇◇◇

1 Man and Crystals

IT has been said that there are few innovations which can truthfully claim to be original and that the majority of modern discoveries are but the rediscovery of former knowledge or experience which is then re-presented to the world at large in a modern manner. This is certainly true of a good deal of our modern technology, particularly that which utilises quartz crystals as its motive force. Although the mists of antiquity still obscure our view of many of the uses our fore-bears found for this humble mineral, a measure of detailed information is slowly beginning to re-surface via many mediumistic channels all over the world, and it would appear that quartz crystals have had a long history of service to mankind.

First used on the fabled continent of Atlantis, quartz crystals swiftly became indispensible to the people of that time who capitalised upon their uncanny capacity to store and to amplify any power source fed into them. In a manner still largely unknown to modern civilisation, they lit their homes and cities utilising large synthetic crystals. These same crystals provided the motivation for their different forms of transport. Modern-day science is slowly beginning to regain some of this lost knowledge and today synthetic crystals are being manufactured upon some of the space shuttles launched by the United States.

During the Atlantean period it was the priesthood who pioneered the development of crystal power, for they utilised their natural electromagnetic energy to effect changes in the mental, physical and spiritual bodies of mankind. During the early epochs of the Atlantean culture, the crystals were left in their natural state, the vast caverns wherein they grew being adapted as healing chambers by the priesthood. These vast crystal formations pulsated with a vibrant energy which the priests tapped in order to bring about a personality change within those who had transgressed their laws.

Leading the offenders within such a cavern, the initiate priests would first select a suitable crystal before positioning the miscreant before it. They would then 'tune-in' to the elemental intelligence of the crystal formation, which responded by releasing a potent electromagnetic energy. The offender was then left to absorb this powerful vibration which served to transmute their negative thought patterns into constructive acts. (The modern-day practice of applying electrodes to the heads of those who suffer from severe depression would appear to reflect this long-forgotten activity.)

At a later point in the Atlantean civilisation these quartz crystals were cut and distributed throughout their many colonies, where they were utilised within their healing hospices, which in themselves often resembled vast engineering stations. Atlantis itself was a volatile continent subject to continual volcanic eruption, requiring the people to adapt their lifestyle accordingly. Tapping into the core of a volcano they drew off its gasses, steam and geothermal waters utilising these to heat their homes and cities.

Among the Atlantean peoples, it was the Toltecs who developed the most perfect of civilisations. The Toltecs used quartz crystals for many purposes. In their temples the priesthood perfected the use of quartz crystals, creating crystal mirrors which enabled specially trained young women to develop latent visionary capacities. They also had an awareness of the beneficial effects of sound and colour, and within their healing chambers they developed a variation of the treatment formerly undertaken within the underground caverns.

Placing offenders—usually those who refused to acknowledge the laws of their society—within a room filled with crystals of every hue and size, a priest would select one crystal, striking this with a small rod before withdrawing. All crystals possess an individual 'note' or 'sound'—a quality they have in common with mankind—and as the crystal released its sound into the ethers, its resonance caused the remaining crystals to respond by releasing their own sound, subsequently filling the chamber with their vibrations. All such vibration creates colour patterns within the ethers and this harmonious combination of sound and colour, coupled with the pulsating electromagnetic energy released by each crystal in turn brought about startling transformations within those who were subjected to it.

The Atlanteans also used quartz crystals for deeply occult purposes, for they were considered to possess a sacred energy. One individual, usually female, would be selected to become Keeper of the Temple Crystal and it was her sole task to ensure that it was never sullied by negative thought patterns or vibrations. As the abuse of thought was by then a major problem throughout Atlantis, this was a major undertaking.

With the appearance on Earth of the Ahriamanic Forces—referred to in the Bible as 'the Sons of Belial'

—the pace of life in Atlantis swiftly altered and those
who fell under Ahriamanic control were subsequently
taught to grow perfect synthetic crystals, for all natural
specimens were ostensibly developed for beneficial
purposes, although all too soon they became weapons
of destruction.

These dark forces capitalised upon the discontent of
the male members of society who grew increasingly
restless, desiring to develop their latent visionary capacities in order to compete with the women who
had, through the use of these abilities, become the
true rulers of Atlantis. Those men who so desired
were taught the art of receiving telepathic messages—
utilising a synthetic crystal as a receiver, in much the
same manner as our current civilisation used the early
crystal radio sets. However, lacking the years of disci-
plined training undergone by their female counter-
parts, the majority of the communications received
related only to third-dimensional situations, in a
manner similar to modern-day fortune telling. Utilising
this information, the Ahriamanic Forces grew ever
stronger.

All manner of mechanical knowledge was then released by these Sons of Belial, who encouraged the
development of gigantic synthetic crystals to power the
many forms of motivation which then came into being
upon the continent of Atlantis. Airships, submarines
and pleasure craft were all powered by large crystal
generators which obtained their energy via lasers projected from specifically designed power stations.

Under the guidance of these dark forces the Toltecs
perfected types of crystals which were capable of at-
tracting the radio-active energies of Stellar Bodies, as
well as other forms of energy located in the ethers
which surround the earth. These powerful energies,
together with the trapped rays of the Sun, were fed

into vast storage crystals and subsequently directed via smaller crystals to the on-board generators of their various forms of transport. In this manner they utilised a form of atomic energy for the benefit of the human race.

Sadly, these powers were all too soon adapted for destructive purposes as the Ahriamanic Forces began to battle with the priesthood for supremacy. The radio-active energies obtained from the solar system were then directed deep into the body of the Earth via specially constructed crystals placed in large underground pits, dug in the vicinity of the major temples of light. In this manner they endeavoured to destroy the temples through the stimulation of earthquake activity, but their blind ignorance of Natural Laws resulted in massive upheavals which subsequently divided the continent into a series of islands. Having failed to dislodge the priests from their point of supremacy, the battles continued and much similarly foolish activity resulted in the total destruction of the Atlantean civilisation and the scattering of its peoples across the face of the Earth.

Prior to all of the major cataclysms, the priesthood caused the purer element of the Atlantean race to flee, setting up replica civilisations in the Americas and in Egypt. According to traditional teachings of the North American Indians, their forefathers came from an island called 'Atlan' in large boats and in their mystical rites made great use of quartz crystals. The present-day Red Indians of North America are said to be the best representatives of the ancient Toltec people.

In Egypt the priest-led colonists attempted to re-create the pure ethic of the Atlantean civilisation and almost succeeded. They brought with them the powerful temple crystals which were then utilised to re-establish harmony between the Heavens and the

Earth—or the Seen and the Unseen. It is said that the great pyramids of Gizeh, together with the Sphynx, were built by the Atlantean colonists before the final cataclysm—or the Great Flood, as it is referred to in all world histories. Those pyramids and the Sphynx were replicas of the great Temple of the Heights in Atlantis, representing their ancient mystery school, and are said to have been constructed utilising the powers of quartz crystals to create weightlessness within the enormous blocks used in their construction. Similar stories relating to the erection of the mighty megalithic structures which are found scattered throughout Great Britain and Northern France today abound.

As the Egyptian culture developed, the priests continued to use the powers of the mineral Kingdom, setting large uncut gemstones within huge golden discs through which they focused the rays of the sun upon the affected portion of a patient's anatomy—a practice they found to be highly beneficial in restoring general well-being.

Quartz crystals were incorporated within all their temple rites, particularly within the Temple of Beauty, wherein training in the healing arts was undertaken. The healer-priests of the early Egyptian culture were well aware that conditions of disease reflected a measure of spiritual imbalance and quartz crystals were used in an endeavour to re-establish harmony between the mind, body and spirit.

Sadly, the Ahriamanic Forces infiltrated this brave new civilisation, once again seeking to gain control of the minds of the people, and to a large extent they succeeded. This time, however, the powers of the Crystal Kingdom were withdrawn from mankind, thus preventing a similar abuse. These Sons of Belial seek total control of mankind, and as they have demonstrated in the past, they are quite prepared to destroy large portions of the planet in an endeavour to achieve their aims. Their power lies within the mechanical knowledge they possess, which they have once again shared with the human race. It is to be hoped that we have seen the light, and will not be foolish enough to repeat the errors made in Atlantis.

Some members of the Atlantean priesthood fled to what is now northern Europe and here they reverted to the simplest form of the Atlantean faith, setting up crude stone formations to serve as their temples. With the passage of time, their occult knowledge was passed from initiate to initiate resulting in what is known today as the Druidic cult of Great Britain and Northern France.

Their knowledge of the harmony between the Heavens and the Earth led them to erect the megalithic structures, stone barrows and cairns which so puzzle many people today. All such constructions served as conductors of the earth energy—known as 'ley power'—which they carried over the countryside, aiding the propagation of crops. This power was also utilised within their fertility rites, enacted within the megalithic circles which were, in themselves, points of great magnetic power.

Following a great deal of scientific study it has been ascertained that the majority of these sites are located close to known geological fault lines, and all minerals located in the vicinity of such faults are subject to a great deal of pressure from time to time.

Among the many minerals located throughout the world is silicon dioxide—or quartz—which is known to be piezo-electric, emitting an electrical charge when pressure is applied to it. Large quantities of quartz crystals are found in the substrata of the Earth beneath all of the known megalithic sites.

A megalithic site

The stone circles which were erected at places such as Stonehenge in the United Kingdom became places of great magnetic power, for the Druids divined that when lintels were placed upon the upright stones, the electrical energies were transferred to the next upright and so on, thereby caging immense forces within those circles. This energy was then utilised in many—still secret—ways, but it is known that it enabled the priests to perform healing miracles and to commune with spirits.

Not surprisingly, these unseen forces still operate within those ancient sites to this day, as I myself discovered when investigating standing stones and cairns in the far north of Scotland some years ago. These forces—appearing to me in the guise of Druids—prevented my entry into one such cairn and upon entering into another, I was advised of their continuing role in the collection and distribution of the mysterious 'ley power' despite our current ignorance of its existence.

Knowledge of the powers of quartz crystals is to be found within the teachings of all races which have retained mystical belief as part of their culture. The Medicine Indians of South America believe crystals to be inhabited by spirits and are therefore considered to be sacred stones. Only those who become initiates within their tribal rites are permitted to view them.

Further evidence of the importance attached to quartz crystals by primitive tribes is reflected in several crystal skulls which have been discovered by archeologists investigating the ruins of ancient Mayan temples. To date five of these have been located, one of which is now in the British Museum in London. Another rests in a museum in Paris. The remainder are all privately owned. These skulls appear to have been carved from the purest quartz crystal and were apparently used in ceremonial rituals, possibly for the purposes of divination. (Indeed, one skull was found to fit perfectly within an indentation upon the altar of the temple wherein it was located.)

The most perfect specimen to date is that discovered early in 1924 by Anna Mitchell-Hedges in a remote Mayan temple in the jungles of British Honduras. According to Toronto journalist Sharon Singer, Anna saw something sparkling beneath a col-

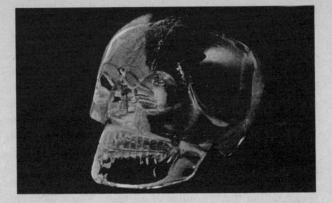

A crystal skull (reproduced by courtesy of the Trustees of the British Museum)

lapsed altar and subsequent excavation unearthed a crystal skull similar to that pictured here.

This is an artifact of great beauty, arousing wonder and reverence in most who view it, despite the fact that Anna's father—the famous archeologist and explorer F. A. Mitchell-Hedges—called it 'the Skull of Doom'! Close examination under powerful microscopes has failed to trace any tool marks upon its highly polished surface, indicating that its unknown creator possessed great lapidary skills, for far from being a solid mass, the skull contains inner light pipes together with prisms and lenses within its eye sockets, and one may only surmise what part it played within temple ceremonials. Scientists today are unable to date it, even by the most modern methods, but it is variously assumed to be between 20,000 and 500,000 years old. Modern-day psychics who have examined it declare that it is a crystal memory bank, containing much ancient knowledge awaiting those who have the ability to decipher its hidden message.

If that sounds far-fetched, consider the experiments which were run some years ago in a derelict old flint-stone building in Wales. For centuries it had served the community as a coaching inn before falling into disuse in recent years. Setting up a series of sensitive record-ing instruments, the investigators placed sensors within the walls and left the machines to record, undisturbed by man. Imagine their surprise when the tapes were played back, for clearly discernible was the sound of human voices, coupled with the everyday sounds of a coaching inn. Flintstone contains a great deal of silicon dioxide—or quartz—a natural recording instrument.

The crystal skulls unearthed to date are intriguing, for few today credit the Mayans with the ability to create such masterpieces. Indeed, it has been stated that these skulls are in fact Atlantean artifacts trans-ported to the Americas by the priesthood prior to the major cataclysms. There is an incredible similarity be-tween the Mayan temple structures and those created by the early Egyptian dynasties, indicating a common link at some point in time.

The Indians of North America considered the powers of quartz crystals to be sacred, and when faced with the problem of sheltered hillsides which received little sunlight, thus preventing the successful growth of crops, they used the powers of crystals in a rather un-usual manner. They would select a large crystal and grind it into small particles, then place these in a large, hollow cow's horn which they then buried in the earth for a year.

When retrieved this resembled a fine crystalline powder, which they then scattered over the hillside in question. At the points where the sun's rays did penetrate, they were magnified, providing light for all crops subsequently planted.

The Aborigines of Australia believed quartz crystals to be magical stones, particularly those which had flaws within them, producing a rainbow effect when light was cast upon them. These they believed contained the Rainbow Spirit who was credited with amazing power, including the destruction of anyone who incurred his wrath.

Throughout time, the right to own a quartz crystal has been restricted to the priesthood and the medicine men of various tribes, as evidenced within the practices of the various Indian tribes of North and South America and the Aborigines of Australia. In this manner their leaders maintained tribal discipline, enforcing unpopular decisions with a measure of 'earth magic'.

In the Far East, the ancient Chinese certainly understood the sacred powers of crystals, and caverns wherein they were located remained undisturbed, guarded by the priests who used them as places of initiation. Both the Japanese and the Chinese have long considered balls of the purest crystal to be talismans aiding contemplation, and venerated them for that purpose.

Finally, a tale which I heard some years ago while lecturing in North America may provide an answer to one of the most intriguing mysteries of modern times. A group of skin divers exploring the sea-bed off the coast of Florida following a storm, discovered a number of buildings there, among them—reputedly —a pyramid structure. The return of bad weather prevented further investigation of this site—it disappeared again beneath mounds of sand and silt.

When they did eventually re-locate this site some two years later, they obtained from the ruins a crystal ball which has three ghost-like pyramids deep within its structure, stated to have the most amazing energy field. Since that time nothing more has been heard of strange occurrences within the area known as the Bermuda Triangle. There may of course be no connection between the two, but it is a rather odd coincidence.

The phase of experience which lies ahead of the human race is challenging, bringing with it the promise of a new Golden Age, reminiscent of the Toltec Era of Atlantis. Mystical truths—which until this point in time have been restricted to neophytes and initiates—will become common knowledge, for each new age develops its own Mysteries. Those who now begin to search for truth or who desire to locate their specific purpose in life will be accorded opportunities to expand their current levels of consciousness and to attain spiritual growth.

The information shared in these pages is but a fragment of the great truths still awaiting us, provided to test the reaction of mankind. Many who read these words are those who—like myself—failed in Atlantis and who have returned to face similar challenges. We must not fail this time, for the Sons of Belial are already among us, offering illusionary materialistic powers. This time we must protect the Mineral Kingdom if we are to save the human race.

◇◇◇◇◇◇◇◇◇◇◇◇◇◇◇◇◇◇◇◇◇◇◇◇◇◇◇

2 A Practical Viewpoint

FRIENDS and associates who have a scientific background look a trifle askance whenever I raise the subject of quartz crystals, for my belief regarding their possession of an elemental intelligence causes grave misgivings as to my level of sanity, particularly when I further state that they respond to love by releasing an electromagnetic energy.

Being scientific in outlook they view such occurrences merely as an energy interchange, and have difficulty in accepting such statements. Yet energy, vibration, and matter are really one and the same, this point being borne out by some modern-day physicists who contend that our physical forms consist of energy —and not matter as had classically been assumed. They also state that all three-dimensional forms are but manifestations of energy, vibrating at a particular rate.

The natural outcome of a flow of energy is the stimulation of activity, but where that energy is not directed or ordered, it disperses and is lost to mankind. A thought pattern of 'love'—in itself a powerful energy —which is directed toward an elemental intelligence

—a pure form of energy—within a quartz crystal, will result in the crystal releasing the electromagnetic forces under its control. This serves as a perfect illustration of ordered energy, which in turn can be utilised to benefit mankind. The electromagnetic force which subsequently permeates the atoms of the etheric body, affecting in turn those of the physical form, comes from the Source of all such energies, that which we term the God-Head.

Despite the foregoing, many still puzzle over how quartz crystals can possibly project an electromagnetic energy, a point which can be illustrated with a simple experiment using wire coils which are capable of carrying an electrical current. Such activity will result in a wide electromagnetic field around the perimeter of that coil, but as this energy is not being directed into any particular field, it soon disperses into the ethers. However, when a soft iron rod is placed in the centre of that coil, the energy is then focused or directed into

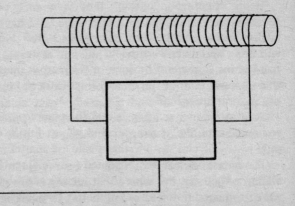

Wire coil and soft iron bar create an electromagnetic field

the rod, which in turn becomes magnetic and will then magnetise any suitable mineral with which it comes into contact.

It is known that there are vast iron ore deposits within the sub-strata of the planet and the iron particles line up north-south whenever they are free to move (when they are molten, for example), attracted as they are to magnetic North and South Poles. They become magnetised in a similar manner to the iron rod within the coil. These magnetised deposits subsequently influence the growth patterns of all minerals within their vicinity, particularly quartz crystals. Where such energies are present during the 'seeding time' of rock quartz—that initial period when the boiling geothermal waters, laden with liquified silicon dioxide, pour through ancient volcanic gas chambers, or flood the fissures deep beneath the Earth's surface—they are absorbed within the structure of the slowly forming crystals.

The closer such crystal formations lie to the magnetic core of the planet, the greater their magnetic field. All quartz mined in areas such as Arkansas in the United States—a region which is extremely close to that core—emit powerful electromagnetic energies, and this area currently provides the purest quartz crystals known to mankind. Much of the output mined in this region is used by the electrical industry to improve our current lifestyle.

Ancient science teaches us that the planet possesses four elements, fire, earth, air and water; but in common with all else within this plane of matter, such elements are themselves ensouled—by elementals—which in their natural state act in, or are activated by, pure or unconditional love. All matter possesses a lifeforce, or as some prefer to term it, intelligence, of some kind, which acts upon constructive direction.

It was Edison who first stated that 'every cell thinks'. Since Edison's day many scientists and medical practitioners have speculated upon the existence of forms of energy within the human brain. Some have developed devices, known as psychotronic generators, to trap and store such energies in a bid to demonstrate, in a practical manner, the hidden powers of the brain. The modern bio-feedback machines, used by some natural healing practitioners today to illustrate how the mind can be trained to control bodily functions, provide yet another illustration of this same energy.

The Indian tribes of North America discovered long ago that projections of a thought pattern of 'love' and 'hatred' result in the release of extremely powerful— but totally different—frequencies of electromagnetic radiation, which is then absorbed by all life-forms within a certain radius. This truth has been proved in scientific experiments which involve the wiring of plants to highly sensitive recording devices which then measured the reactions of the plants to both emotions.

When we project loving thoughts towards a quartz crystal, the pure vibrations we emit are absorbed within the energy field of that crystal and, being a positive vibration, the response will be an almost instantaneous release of its electromagnetic energies. Those who merely hold a crystal and do not attempt to project a thought pattern or mental image toward it, will, on the other hand, experience little in the way of energy interchange.

Contrary to generally held belief, quartz crystals are not energised by the Sun, although they can be utilised to concentrate its rays. It is the Moon which stimulates the energy field of a quartz crystal, for as it is drawn ever closer by the gravitational pull of the Earth—as happens at the time of the full moon—its close proximity stimulates all magnetic fields.

The inbuilt electromagnetic properties of quartz crystals are therefore intensified during such periods, and quartz formations then begin to emit very potent forces, particularly during the hours of night. A clear quartz crystal in the bedroom at the time of the full moon will cause all in the room to experience a great deal of painful pressure in the region of the crown of the head, pressure which subsides only when the offending crystal is removed from the room.

As the Moon begins to wane the energy flow from quartz crystals is far less potent, for as it is released from the pull of the Earth, its influence upon Earth's structures becomes noticeably weaker, resulting in a marked decrease in the outflow of electromagnetic energy.

Rock quartz is the most structured of the mineral species, possessing a high and very exact rate of vibration, making it invaluable to modern technology. This very precise rate of vibration can be utilised to transform rates of vibration in other substances, hence its beneficial effects upon human energy fields.

Most organic crystals, however, are invariably flawed in some way, causing the quartz to shatter when an electrical charge is fed into them. In seeking to overcome this problem, American scientists are planning to manufacture crystals at the projected space station which is scheduled to become operational in the early 1990s. In this manner they will create perfect crystals, free from flaws, for use in future scientific projects.

3 The Ascended Masters

WE live in a hierarchical society, a pattern of life mankind has happily accepted throughout time, apart from some notable exceptions in recent years. Within it, information relating to decisions taken by elected governments filters through the structured layers of society to the ordinary men and women who form the majority in any land, who are then expected to act accordingly.

As the human race has evolved through countless civilisations, certain individuals have striven to perfect themselves, mastering their base emotions whilst seeking to serve mankind in some manner. Such individuals have emerged to the forefront in historical undertakings and with due testing have become what are termed today 'the Ascended Masters'.

Despite many claims to the contrary, our physical forms are ensouled by a spiritual force which has its origin within that force of Divine Love which we term 'God'. This spiritual force is the reincarnating entity which seeks perfection through repeated physical embodiments. As such we must also acknowledge and endeavour to carry out decisions which have been made

21

in the Spiritual Parliament, whose representatives are the Ascended Masters.

To these Brothers of Light are accorded tasks which relate to the continued evolution of the human race coupled with the expansion of our levels of consciousness. A new age dawns, bringing with it many fresh challenges for all concerned.

The world-wide re-awakening of awareness of the benefits which accrue from the use of quartz crystals is largely due to the combined efforts of two of these Illumined Souls, The Master Ragoczy, better known to the world as the Comte de St Germain, and the Master Djwal Khul, also known as The Tibetan Master.

Together they seek to re-activate conscious awareness of the true Self—that which is termed 'the Spirit Reality'—coupled with an understanding of the life-force which permeates all matter. All life-forms currently undergoing physical experience within this three-dimensional world are interdependent and until this truth is accepted, we will all remain trapped within vain illusion.

The major task which currently confronts mankind lies in the necessity to undergo a change in consciousness, the overall goal being to develop awareness of the Fourth Dimension—otherwise termed 'the Spiritual Plane'—and to relate to it in much the same manner as we currently do to the illusionary three dimensions of matter.

To aid this eventuality the Illumined Beings discussed here are currently re-activating former knowledge relating to the use of colour, sound and the Mineral Kingdom. All sound emanating from physical forms results in a form of vibration within the ethers which surround us. This in turn creates colour patterns which subsequently affect our everyday thought and action. When both sound and colour are absorbed within the Mineral Kingdom—but in particular by quartz crystals—it results in an intensification of the electromagnetic energies such structures emit. These in turn are absorbed by the vegetable, animal and human forms, thereby stimulating growth and aiding the expansion of consciousness upon the various levels of experience.

The Master Ragoczy has long aided the advancement of mankind, from an early lifetime as the Chinese Philosopher Lao Tze, to the legendary Merlin at

The Master Ragoczy

the court of King Arthur. In later times He influenced the Elizabethan culture, where He appeared as Francis Bacon and, more recently, as the Comte de St Germain, He sought to bring about many necessary reforms throughout eighteenth-century Europe.

He particularly concentrates His energies within the field of sound, seeking to influence those musicians who are in any way sensitive to New Age energies, encouraging the composition of muted and melodic harmonies which in turn will assist with the introduction of new pastel hues into our colour spectrum.

The Master Djwal Khul focuses much of His attention upon those who seek to perfect the ethics of healing and, in particular, aiding those who seek to

The Master Djwal Khul

develop new methods of treating the sick. He also endeavours to bring about awareness of the necessity for a return to balance and harmony within our everyday lives, the lack of which has led to the great upsurge in psychosomatic disorders, particularly within the Western world.

In the process of restoring to mankind a measure of awareness of the immense potential for universal betterment which currently lies dormant within the Mineral Kingdom, these Illumined Ones also aid the indwelling intelligence of that kingdom, encouraging the desire to free itself from its crystaline world. In this manner the inhabitants of both kingdoms evolve in accordance with the Divine Plan.

◇◇◇◇◇◇◇◇◇◇◇◇◇◇◇◇◇◇◇◇◇◇◇◇◇◇◇◇◇◇◇

4   Children of the Earth

ROCK crystals are the children of the Earth itself, having formed slowly and laboriously deep beneath the surface of the planet, in much the same manner as a child forms within the womb. They have their origin within the restless, molten magma of the Earth's core, which is ever seeking to reach the outer surface. However, only a very small proportion of this fiery mass results in volcanic activity and lava flow, the majority of the magma flowing instead through the subterranean fissures and crevasses which honeycomb the substrata of the planet.

This mass of molten rock and minerals is accompanied by boiling waters, steam and gasses, which, as they cool, begin to form into crystals, building upon the many minerals deposited within those fissures. In this manner do rock crystals and gemstones begin their development, slowly forming their light in the primeval darkness, taking perhaps 20 to 30 million years to achieve any real size.

All three-dimensional forms currently undergoing growth experiences upon or within this world of matter possess a life energy of one kind or another, and ele-

mental forces inhabit the developing crystalline structures, overseeing their growth, slowly creating a world
of their own. Despite the limits placed upon their development by the narrow confines of those fissures, a
great deal of ingenuity is demonstrated by those
forces, who carefully adjust the growth patterns of the
varying crystalline structures to ensure that all attain
the maximum level of individual expansion. This often
results in what are termed 'clusters' of crystals, with a
number of elementals being gathered together within
one powerful grouping.

In common with children of all ages, rock crystals
will readily respond to loving attention and, in return,
will provide those who care for them with an endless
supply of electromagnetic energy. This vitalising force
will stimulate the energy levels of all individuals who
happen to be in the vicinity of the crystal, leading in
turn to a spiritual quickening and raising of levels of
consciousness.

Gentle, harmonious music also produces a ready response from the indwelling elemental, and the combination of sound and loving thought stimulates a desire
to become a part of the 'outer' world, thereby aiding
its evolution. Once free of the rigid confines of the
Mineral Kingdom, it may then progress towards fresh
experience and expression within the Plant or Vegetable Kingdom.

Many who read these words may well doubt such
statements, or refuse to accept the truth that apparently inanimate matter possesses an energy which is
capable of progression to another phase of experience.

The following might provide such individuals with
food for thought. Whilst holding a much-loved crystal
recently, I gazed at an oddly shaped cluster of crystals
upon a nearby shelf, and contemplated the possibility
of breaking this in two, creating from it two reasonably

shaped clusters. The elemental intelligence within that quartz formation immediately voiced its alarm at my intention, conveying this via the crystal within my hand. The resulting shock waves did not subside until I mentally assured the indwelling intelligence of the misshapen cluster that I would not break it up.

Astounding as this may appear to be, it is really quite simple to explain. Thought patterns create an energy which is amplified within the structure of a quartz crystal. My idle thoughts were picked up by my personal crystal, duly amplified and projected into the ethers, where they were received by the intelligence within the said quartz formation. Its alarmed response was transmitted in the same manner, echoed by the crystal within my hand and reflected as shock waves within my body.

Similar reactions have been noted in scientifically conducted experiments with plants which were wired to very sensitive monitoring devices. Some plants were shown a great deal of attention, others were ignored and one was abused. Whenever the person who had abused the plant entered the room, all of the plants registered alarm upon the measuring devices.

Intelligence of some kind exists upon all levels, and simple experimentation by my readers with crystals or plants will certainly prove this point, provided of course, that one is sensitive to finer forces.

5 Quartz Formations

WHEN first investigating the benefits which arise
from association with the Mineral Kingdom, one is
often faced with a bewildering array of rock crystals of
varying hues and sizes, and most individuals are perplexed as to which would prove to be the most suitable
for their purposes.

Many incorrectly assume that all rock crystals,
being of the same species of quartz, will perform in
much the same manner, no matter what their size, colour or shape. This is a common misunderstanding, but
just as no two individuals—even members of the same
family—will react in a similar manner to identical situations, rock crystals perform in an individualistic way,
each possessing separate identities and qualities.

Experimentation with a number of crystals is therefore advisable, in order that one may ascertain just
which crystal will provide the greatest assistance for
the tasks one wishes to undertake. The size of the
crystal can be, but is not necessarily important—nei-
ther is it indicative of its energy level, for some of the
small, very clear crystals emit a potent force.

In common with mankind, each individual crystal
possesses a naturally corresponding 'note' or 'sound'.
When selecting a personal crystal it is by means of this
inaudible note that we are drawn towards any particular crystal. The indwelling elemental, recognising your
personal note of sound in the higher ethers, attracts
your attention by projecting its own special sound in
those same ethers. In this we recognise the Law of
Attraction and Repulsion at work, and this is clearly
noticeable whenever a group of individuals are

endeavouring to locate 'their' crystal within a large collection offered for sale.

The crystals which attract the greatest attention are the 'positive' or 'masculine' variety, for they possess great clarity. Indeed, such crystals often emit the most intense energies, making them potent instruments in the field of natural healing.

The masculine crystal, due to its level of clarity, will provide positive assistance for those who are somewhat confused, their overall view of life clouded by emotion. Where such individuals can be persuaded to focus their attention upon such a crystal, it will enable them to acquire a much clearer outlook upon life, aiding the release of their pent-up emotions.

Equally, for those who desire to go beyond the mind within their meditative practices, these crystals provide a powerful stimulus for the chakra system, enabling one to attain the desired goal.

Exposure to positive or masculine crystals results in activity, and such quartz formations are of benefit where stimulus or action is required, particularly in situations where physical exhaustion is a problem. The introduction of this positive force into one's etheric or electromagnetic field swiftly restores low or weakened energy levels.

Rock quartz is a mineral which is closely allied to the energies of the Moon, whose effect upon sensitive individuals is well known. Indeed, the energy flow of a crystal will appear to ebb and flow in accordance with the phases of the Moon, reaching a peak when the Moon is full.

Should one desire to activate latent mediumistic qualities, a cluster of feminine quartz crystals will swiftly accelerate one's spiritual momentum by activating those chakra centres which relate to intuition and clairvoyance. The feminine varieties of quartz are often rather ugly, being cloudy or opaque in their appearance, but do nonetheless possess unique properties.

Whenever one is suffering from the effects of an overabundance of mental, emotional or physical activity, resulting in painful headaches or migraine, a feminine crystal will help to reduce the tensions caused by such over-activity. This is achieved by holding the crystal in the right hand, with its point directed towards the area of stress. Place the left hand in the region of the Thyroid Chakra, or, if preferred, in the region of the Solar Plexus Chakra, and concentrate upon the projection of a thought pattern of 'love' to the elemental of the crystal. Within a short period of time, the pain will ease, and some ten minutes of such activity should free one from pain completely.

We are all partly male and partly female, but all too often we restrict expression of that aspect of our dual natures which is not considered to be natural. Those who experience difficulty in relating to the feminine or sensitive aspect of their nature, should seek to acquire and use a milky or cloudy crystal in their daily routine. As we progress toward the Age of Aquarius, unrestricted expression of the feminine principle—regardless of our gender—becomes vital, for it is an age within which the use of the inner or spiritual senses will receive a great deal of attention.

A cluster formation of rock quartz crystals is today considered to be a collector's item, and such structures do command extremely high prices. Many are a combination of masculine and feminine crystals, although it is often possible to acquire clusters which are completely masculine in their energies. These are extremely beautiful, but do possess very potent force-fields, providing powerful stimulus for those who are engaged in natural healing practices. The totally

Masculine crystal

A cluster of feminine crystals

feminine crystals, on the other hand, should be sought by those who are in search of spiritual horizons or who desire to develop visionary talents.

Such formations are extremely powerful generators of electromagnetic energies, which in turn serve to strengthen the etheric field of anyone who happens to be in their vicinity. The larger the cluster, the greater their force-field, which in itself is extremely protective of those within its charge.

It is possible to obtain very large formations of crystals—some stand three feet high with a similar circumference—and extreme caution should be exercised when siting these within the home. Indeed, the wise among you will ensure that such structures are placed well away from the general sleeping quarters. Those who fail to heed this advice can expect to experience extreme pressure and pain in the region of the head during the early hours of the morning, for the rock crystals are stimulated anew at such times, by the energies of the Moon. The crystal formation will then proceed to carry out its allotted task, namely, that of releasing its newly replenished force into the ethers for use on higher levels of consciousness.

Those energies invariably activate the Crown Chakra of any individual who happens to be within its radius. The resulting pain is quite unbearable and its effects often last for several hours.

Such activity forms part of the natural role of the group of elementals within that cluster formation, who endeavour to increase the level of spiritual awareness within those who have shared 'love' with them. Although such activity is greatly beneficial for the recipient in the long term, the initial effects can prove to be somewhat disturbing.

For those who are engaged in natural healing practices, I recommend placing each hand in turn within

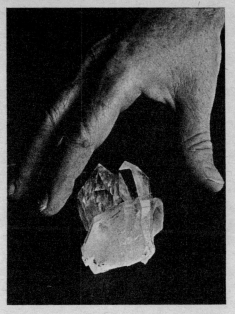

the energy field of a cluster formation for several minutes prior to the healing act, for this serves to stimulate the chakras or sensors within the hands, thereby intensifying one's level of sensitivity, whilst increasing the overall benefits to the recipient.

Known as 'the mirror of the Seer', crystal balls have long been known to possess the ability to reflect visionary patterns for those who are gifted in this way. They are in fact a derivative of the crystal mirrors once used in Atlantis, where flat mirrors carved from the purest crystal were utilised by the temple virgins.

A cautionary note. Should your visionary ability be activated only when you close your eyes, then the crystal ball will serve no valid purpose. Only those who are able to 'perceive' other dimensions whilst their

physical eyes are focused upon the crystal ball, will derive any benefit from their use.

Lead Crystal

This form of crystal is currently enjoying a great deal of popularity, and can be obtained either as prisms or pendants, the latter (due to their beauty) being favoured by the ladies. However, such crystals offer no constructive benefits, for they contain only those energies which were present in the ethers at the time of their manufacture.

Those who wear such crystals will naturally imbue them with their own electromagnetic energies, but as they are not naturally formed, they do not contain a 'life-force' of their own. Therefore, unlike natural rock crystals, they gain no benefit from the energies of the Moon, and do not absorb the electromagnetic energies which flow through the ethers. Although attractive,

Lead crystal

lead crystals offer no assistance to the natural healer, or to the would-be visionary.

Smokey Quartz

This is a very powerful form of rock quartz, and great care should be exercised when handling it. All quartz formations absorb within their structure, the energies which are present in their environment during their growth period. Within certain subterranean regions of this planet there exist naturally occurring radio-active materials which greatly affect the structure of minerals such as rock quartz. The close proximity of such materials results in an intensified energy field, whilst its original clarity is lost, as it takes on a grey/brown hue.

Exposure to smokey quartz will therefore result in a similar level of intensification within the subtle bodies of mankind. In turn this will prove to be of great benefit to those who seriously desire to acquire full fourth-dimensional awareness or to attune to their Greater Self.

Within the dense physical form, these stimulating energies will aid the release of all mental and emotional tensions, making this a powerful healing stone when handled wisely. Single crystals of the smokey quartz variety project a potent force; indeed, tests have shown them to generate a greater energy than many medium-sized clusters of quartz crystals.

They should therefore be utilised only in situations which call for powerful stimulus, such as when energy levels are greatly depleted following surgery. In such cases, a single smokey quartz crystal should be placed at the feet of the individual concerned whilst a healing treatment is carried out.

The energies projected by this irradiated variety of quartz are often overpowering, resulting in reactions which range from powerful pressure upon the chakra points, to palpitations of the heart. Where the latter condition is noted, it is advisable to remove the smokey quartz crystal from the immediate vicinity.

Amethyst Quartz

Amethyst quartz crystals are much prized due to their great beauty, but possess potent energies which make them indispensible to New Age healers and therapists. When placed within the treatment room, such clusters will emit a powerful, purifying energy, stimulating to both healer and the individual in need of treatment.

Although the energy fields of such clusters may appear to be less potent than those projected by similarly sized clusters of rock quartz, the benefits that accrue from the use of amethyst quartz in healing treatments is immeasurable. In particular, the energy generated by such clusters has a beneficial effect upon the nervous system, providing healing therapists with a positive aid when endeavouring to treat related conditions.

When suffering from irritating skin disorders, an amethyst cluster placed (point downward) upon the affected region, will soon bring relief; or for those who experience painful eye conditions, the cluster held an inch or two from the eyes will—when stimulated by a thought pattern of 'love'—result in the release of a laser-like ray of healing energy, which in turn will ease the tension within the eyes.

The amethyst hue of this variety of quartz reflects the purest aspect of the violet ray, one of several shades of colour which will greatly influence mental and spiritual outgrowth during the New Age. The amethyst shade of colour is extremely powerful, containing as it does all other colours of the spectrum within its make-up, but being such a pure shade, its energies are capable of permeating matter. The healer will therefore find amethyst quartz an invaluable aid when

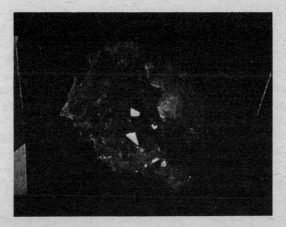

Amethyst Quartz

endeavouring to counteract the effects of negative thought patterns, such as fear or apprehension.

When working in close proximity to clusters of amethyst quartz for any length of time, the energy they emit will lead to the stimulation of one's Crown Chakra—that point within one's energy field where spiritual inspiration is received as a kaleidoscope of constantly changing colour and symbols. Those using such mineral specimens must therefore be prepared to undergo a measure of painful activity within the upper regions of the head, pain which, although beneficial in the long term, can prove to be a somewhat uncomfortable experience. Where the resulting level of pain prevents one from fulfilling everyday tasks, it is suggested that a feminine or milky quartz crystal be held above the Crown Chakra, and the left hand placed in the vicinity of the Thyroid Chakra, whilst the mind projects a thought pattern of 'love' to the crystal elemental. The gentle energies of the feminine crystal will swiftly calm any over-activity stimulated by the amethyst quartz, permitting resumption of routine tasks.

Finally, due to the purifying effect of its energy field, an amethyst cluster may be utilised to cleanse rock crystals of the negative vibrations they absorb when they play a part within the healing act. At day's end, place the crystals upon the amethyst cluster and leave overnight. Next morning they may be used once more in one's healing ministrations, their structure now free of all disharmonious vibrations.

At least once a week, physically clean your amethyst cluster of the accumulation of dust and whatever vibrations it may have absorbed in the course of such tasks. Place it in a saline solution overnight, rinsing the following morning in warm water, before gently placing it, up-ended, to drain. Your cluster will once more be bright, shining and ready to continue its role on your behalf. Do remember that the indwelling inhabitants of your cluster will readily respond to the projection of love coupled with the sound of gentle music, resulting in a positive outflow of vibrant electromagnetic energy.

6   Cleansing a Crystal

HAVING selected a rock crystal suitable for one's requirements, it is necessary to take certain preparatory steps before it is put to use within whatever practice one has obtained this for, the primary task being the physical cleansing of the crystal.

When these are first mined, they are often encrusted with various forms of mineral matter which is removed by placing the crystals in a bath of oxalic acid. From that point onward, the crystals are handled by numerous individuals, each in turn leaving their own mental or emotional imprint upon them.

To eradicate such unwanted vibrations, together with any residue of oxalic acid, it is recommended that the crystal be immersed within natural sea salt for several days. This will absorb whatever vibrations there are upon the crystal, whilst cleansing it of any chemical residue. Quite often, a crystal will emerge from its bed of sea salt sparkling, bright and clear, earlier imperfections having been removed by the reaction of the salt crystals upon its structure.

The crystal should then be rinsed in cold, clear water before undertaking the second stage of its preparation for use. Do not allow others to handle the crystal from this point on, for they will subconsciously impregnate this with their own thoughts or desires, resulting in the need to purify the crystal once more.

If using the crystal daily, it will need to be immersed in a saline solution once a week to remove any negative vibrations it may have absorbed. (Extreme care should be exercised with regard to the level of one's thought patterns whilst working with rock quartz, for they will be magnified by the energies of the crystal, leading quite often to disastrous results.)

Place a tablespoon of sea salt in a small glass bowl filled with warm water and ensure that this is totally dissolved before immersing the crystal. Leave overnight and rinse in cold water the following morning.

The crystal is now ready for re-activation and to resume the role you have programmed it to undertake.

For those who are reluctant to be separated from their newly acquired crystals for several days while they undergo the necessary cleansing process, a recently discovered method might be preferable, particularly as it greatly accelerates the overall process.

Fill a glass container with two pints of warm water and add to it two tablespoons of sea salt, plus two tablespoons of cider vinegar. Once the sea salt has dissolved, place your crystal into the solution for some 10 minutes before rinsing under cold water. The combined action of the cider vinegar and the sea salt upon quartz crystals is quite remarkable, swiftly removing any unwanted residue from the crystals concerned. Should one have several crystals in need of cleansing, the measures quoted above can be increased up to, say, a cup of cider vinegar and sea-salt to a gallon of water, particularly if one has large cluster formations in need of cleansing.

Do please dispose of the residue, for it contains unwanted energies and vibrations which one would not
wish to transfer to other crystal formations.

7 Activating a Crystal

FROM all forms of natural rock quartz flows a continual stream of electromagnetic energy, which is released into the atmosphere to benefit all life forms. This task is unconsciously undertaken by their elemental inhabitants who are blissfully unaware of 'outer' experiences, caught up as they are within their own crystalline world.

Those of you who desire to capitalise upon this source of power must first dedicate the crystal, together with its indwelling inhabitant, to Universal Purpose, for in so doing you convey to the elemental intelligence a measure of awareness of the higher or 'outer' planes of experience. In turn it will desire to become part of that 'outer' world and, like a chick seeking to break free of its shell, will release ever-increasing levels of electromagnetic energy in its bid to free itself of its crystalline form. Thus the process of evolution continues.

Holding the crystal, point upward, in the left hand, adjacent to the Heart Chakra—the seat of Unconditional Love—project towards the crystal a thought pattern of 'love' for some five minutes. This simple act

49

will establish a rapport between you and the elemental, for the emotion of unconditional love possesses the highest and purest of vibrations, to which the atoms and molecules of the crystalline structure pose no real barrier.

In response, the indwelling elemental will release via the point of the crystal, a tingling flow of electromagnetic energy, easily discernible within the region of the chakras. More often than not, it is the sensitive Throat Chakra which picks up this energy flow, but at times the Brow or Crown Chakras are also stimulated by this initial release of crystalline power.

Continue the projection of 'love' for a further five minutes, noting the increased level of response from one's younger 'brother' or 'sister' within the crystal, who is delighting in this loving contact. The cool stimulating force of the electromagnetic flow will become more pronounced, making one aware, in part at least, of one's own outer energy field and of the benefits which accrue from the introduction of electromagnetic energy into it.

Some among you may well feel a little apprehensive at the thought of introducing an 'outer' energy into one's body, fearing its long-term effects. However, the negative emotion of fear is in itself a destructive force which adversely affects the human glandular system, leading in turn to a depletion of the vital energy within the etheric form, which is our first line of defence against virus-borne diseases.

Whenever power of any kind is introduced into one's subtle or outer bodies, the Spirit Guardian or Doorkeeper is always at hand, closely observing the activity, ensuring that no harm comes to their charge. The crystalline energy of the rock crystal is being acti-

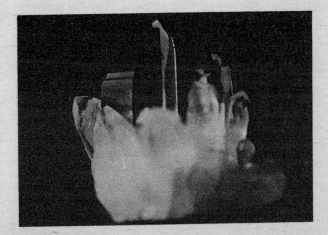

vated by unconditional love and must therefore produce only positive results.

Provided that the crystal is reactivated with a thought pattern of 'love' each and every day, it will, in common with all living things, respond accordingly and fulfil the tasks you programme it to undertake.

Do, however, ensure that no other person handles your crystal, for their thought patterns and/or desires will be communicated to the elemental, who will in turn erase all earlier programmes. The crystal will then need to be cleansed in a saline solution and subsequently re-activated with 'love', as well as with a new programme.

When using rock quartz crystals, it is very important that we fully understand just how powerful thought is. When charged with emotion, thought patterns are exceptionally creative, and as thought is our only means of communicating with the elemental intelligence within the crystal, it is vital to ensure that at such times one's thought patterns are always positive and constructive. Hence the necessity to guard your crystal from the influence of those individuals whose emotions may not be under control, or who may covet your crystal.

To ensure full activation of a quartz crystal and the complete co-operation of the indwelling elemental energy, I suggest you dedicate your crystal in the following manner:

I dedicate this crystal
to Universal Purpose.
From this moment on,
I undertake to utilise
its energies to benefit
all living things.
For I am One with the
Creative Source and
therefore One with all
life forms.
In that which I am, I
now activate the life
energy within this
crystal in order that its
force may now be
utilised to serve
Universal Purpose.

8 Programming Crystals

As natural quartz crystals are known to possess an ability to record and retain memory of any thought pattern which is fed into them, your personal crystal may be programmed in any way you choose. For those who wish to use the crystalline energy for a number of different purposes, it may prove beneficial to gather a small collection of rock crystals and to programme each in turn for a specific task.

To enable the elemental intelligence to carry out your wishes, the crystal will require an input of mental imagery, a task which is relatively simple in itself. Should one wish to utilise a crystal to release muscular or nervous tension, select a clear, masculine crystal and project towards it the image of an expanding spring—as shown in the illustration appearing on page 00. To this should be added the instruction 'release all tension'. From that moment on, the crystal will function as instructed, always provided that one also projects a thought pattern of 'love' toward the elemental before use.

For those who wish to remember dreams or sleep activity, a milky or feminine crystal should be selected,

A feminine quartz cluster

activated with 'love' and dedicated to Universal Purpose. The mental image of a blackboard upon which the words 'record all dream activity' are very clearly written, must be then projected into the crystal, coupled with the instruction 'from this point on record all dream activity when instructed.'

The crystal may then be placed under one's pillow, taking care to activate it with the instruction 'record my dream activity'.

If, on awakening, you have vague memories of a special experience, the details of which elude you, take out the crystal from beneath the pillow—hold it in your right hand—and command the elemental to release all dream memory patterns. As it follows your command, the energies of the crystal will re-activate memory of the experience undergone in the sleep state, and it is advisable to set the details down immediately, for once they have been removed from the crystal's memory bank, they will be lost to you.

On being presented with a feminine crystal recently, a somewhat sceptical associate decided to test this theory for herself, greatly doubting its ability to achieve such a task.

Awakening around 2 a.m., she had partial memory of an incredible journey to higher planes of consciousness during sleep. Grasping her crystal firmly in her right hand, she sleepily commanded that it replay the whole of the dream experience, and to her astonishment, knowledge of the entire night's happenings began to re-assemble within her mind, enabling her to then record this for posterity.

On occasion we have all experienced an inability to sleep, tossing and turning throughout the night, until we observe the dawning of a new day with sheer frustration. Quite by chance recently, I discovered the remarkable ability of a large feminine crystal I possess, to stimulate deep and refreshing sleep. Being overtired due to a long day behind an exhibition stand, I began to despair of ever getting to sleep, when I remembered the crystal sitting on a shelf in another room. Placing it beneath my pillow, I remember little beyond the next 10 minutes. Since that time I have used this crystal constantly, always to great effect.

'Is this possible?' many ask—but sleeplessness is very often caused by an over-active mind and an imbalance within the circulatory system. A feminine crystal will counter the effects of over-activity within the body, resulting in deep and refreshing sleep.

One word of warning, however: do not take masculine or clear crystals into sleeping quarters, for their powers are extremely potent during the hours of darkness, when they are stimulated by the energies of the Moon. This will result in a very restless night for all

concerned, for they will proceed to activate the Crown
Chakra of any individual within that room. This can
prove to be an extremely painful process, particularly
for those in whom this spiritual centre is dormant. Intense pressure will be exerted upon the top of the
head, leading to unbearable levels of pain. Although
beneficial in the long term, few really care for this
form of spiritual therapy during the hours of the night.

9 Chakra Purification

THOUGHT is an extremely potent force and if individuals make no attempt to control everyday thought patterns, they can create havoc in their lives. During the course of everyday events we all, at some point in time, encounter situations or individuals whose express purpose appears to be to frustrate our desires.

One reaction to such encounters is all too often one of resentment, anger, or stubborn refusal to co-operate. The negative energies released into the ethers in this manner swiftly affect our glandular system, which is in turn linked to the chakras, those reception points for spiritual energies located within the Etheric Form.

These highly sensitive centres then become blocked, leading to a loss of those beneficial colour rays which they absorb from the higher ethers. Unless this blockage is removed, it will result in an intensification of the state of negativity—and ill health.

It is therefore recommended that we follow an extremely simple exercise, which will not only serve to cleanse the chakra centres, but also clearly illustrate the power of thought, leading—hopefully—to an ability to control this volatile force in the future.

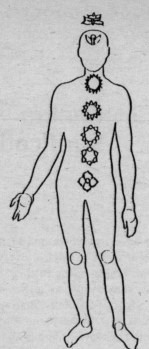

Chakra points

Within those civilisations which retained mystical belief as part of their culture, would-be initiates were always taught to use quartz crystals to cleanse these centres of light. The reasoning behind this act is not too difficult to grasp, for if negative thought patterns can block these spiritual centres, then a positive counter thought, fed through a quartz crystal into the chakras, must surely eradicate any disharmony.

Rock quartz will amplify any energy which is fed into it—and a thought pattern of 'light' is a potent energy. This in turn will be intensified within the struc-

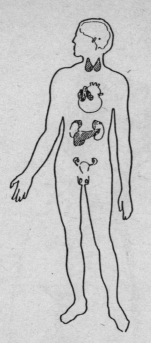

Pineal
Pituitary

Thyroid

Thymus

Adrenals
Pancreas

Gonads

The Endocrine System

ture of the quartz crystal, transforming any negativity within the chakras into light.

A word of warning at this point. In undertaking such an act do not use large quartz crystals or clusters of crystals, for they will release too great an energy into these extremely sensitive centres, and this could lead to even greater problems. A small single crystal, about 2 inches (5 cm) in length is preferable.

Commence this exercise at the Crown Chakra, for this major centre of light is linked to the pituitary gland—known as the Master Gland—which governs

Crown Chakra

the level of activity within the entire endocrine system.
With harmony restored to this centre of light, harmony
will be swiftly reflected within the glandular system,
leading to the restoration of bodily health.

Hold the crystal in the right hand some 3 or 4 inches
(7–10 cm) above the crown of the head, and project a
thought pattern of 'light' through the crystal into the
chakra itself, slowly rotating the crystal as you do so.

The subsequent release of intensified light into this highly sensitive centre may result in searing pain that may last for some considerable time. Despite this, maintain the projection of light for several minutes until you are pressed to move on.

Activation of this reception point for inspiration from the higher mental planes will result in an eventual flood of constantly changing colour and symbolic patterns, which marks the dawning of true clairvoyant vision.

In many individuals, this centre is dormant, for thought begets action, and all too often our path to truth is blocked by the rigid dogmas we absorb during our journey through life. Such individuals may well need to experience a great deal of painful stimulus within this centre before any meaningful activity becomes visible.

Having ascertained that this centre is sufficiently cleansed and fully activated, move the crystal to the second centre and repeat this action.

This is the Brow Chakra, the mystical Third Eye, which in turn is linked to the pineal gland. Little is known of the true purpose of this gland, but it does serve to regulate the emotion of fear, and assists in the maintenance of our bodily cycles. Imbalance within this gland often leads to overstimulation of the gonads.

Do not be surprised if the focus of the crystalline force upon this centre results in a sharp or stabbing pain within the centre of the brow, or at the very least, a sense of irritation, for few today can truly claim that this centre is functioning as it should. (In the Atlantean civilisation the initiates wore gemstones over this centre to further intensify its activity, but the focus of the energy of a small crystal upon this centre will bring about the desired level of activity.)

Brow Chakra

Rotate the crystal, maintaining the projection of the
thought pattern of 'light', until you feel this to be a
fully active centre, tingling with the inflow of electromagnetic energy. The crown and brow chakras are
linked, together forming our psychic camera, providing semi-visual communication with higher realms.
The overall benefits arising from the cleansing and
stimulation of these two important centres lie in a
new-found ability to receive constructive direction for
self and others, which, provided that it is followed, will
lead to spiritual growth and the expansion of consciousness.

The next centre is perhaps the most sensitive of all
and is alternatively known as the throat centre or the
Thyroid Chakra. It is the seat of our sixth sense—that
which we term intuition or clairaudience—and those
among you who have activated this centre possess the

Thyroid Chakra

capacity to 'hear' those telepathic communications which originate upon higher planes of consciousness. (The Atlanteans grew special crystals to undertake this task, but still required human channels to translate the messages.)

The gland to which this centre is linked is one of the Master Glands and in itself controls metabolism. Its activity is very easily disturbed by negative thought patterns such as worry, fear or resentment, which in turn will result in the restriction of the flow of its hormone thyroxine, upon which the body is dependent.

One may need to spend a great deal of time cleansing this chakra in the light of our tendency to worry over inconsequentials. But no matter how long it may take, do maintain the focus of light upon this centre, for your future could depend upon your ability to receive telepathic communication via this centre.

Heart Chakra.

Transfer the crystal to the centre of the breast where the Heart Chakra is located and begin once more to cleanse and activate this centre by the projection of a thought pattern of 'light'. Very few individuals today function through this centre, for it is the seat of the Spirit Self, and is the point from which unconditional love flows. When this point of light becomes active, we begin to develop a measure of Christ Consciousness.

The gland to which this centre is linked, the thymus, forms part of the lymphatic system, and governs physical growth whilst overseeing the development of our sexuality. Its other function appears to lie in developing the body's resistance to infection, by stimulating the formation of the necessary antibodies. The development of allergies clearly indicates a level of imbalance in the thymus gland, as does a lack of bodily growth.

As you feel the stimulating energies of the crystal penetrate this centre, focus your attention upon it, releasing a rose pink ray from deep within. This shade of colour represents Christ Consciousness, a radiant love free of all desire for return. This too will be amplified by the quartz crystal, bringing positive benefits in its wake.

Moving from the seat of the Spirit Self to that of the lower will or ego, we locate within the solar plexus, a difficult chakra to cleanse and balance, given our ten-

Solar Plexus Chakra

dency to follow the dictates of the lower will. This centre is closely allied to the Root Chakra—the seat of the lower nature—and imbalance in one of these centres is invariably reflected within the other. In turn, both centres are influenced by activity within the thyroid chakra, which in itself is easily blocked by negative thought patterns.

The solar plexus therefore is affected by inner and outer disturbances and a sudden shock can inhibit its activity, creating in turn a disturbance within the digestive tract. Whenever we attempt to locate greater self awareness and undertake a measure of spiritual outgrowth, the egoic self retaliates. This conflict between the higher and lower wills is reflected in great tension within this most sensitive of centres.

The gland to which it is linked is the pancreas, part of whose activity deals with the production of two very important hormones, insulin and glucagon. Imbalance within this gland can lead to sudden weight changes, anxiety and disturbances of the stomach.

Focus the energy of the crystal upon this chakra, and note your reaction to the projection of light as the intensified force penetrates this miniature cosmos. As tensions begin to recede and the chakra begins to pulse with the vitalising energy, move on to the next centre requiring attention.

Situated just below the solar plexus is the sacral centre, sometimes referred to as the spleen chakra. This is the seat of compassion in mankind, and is also the point which activates our ability to serve as a healing channel. As so many caring individuals tend to become caught up in the emotional problems of those they endeavour to assist—thereby greatly reducing the benefits of such activity—the Spleen Chakra often requires a deal of attention.

Spleen (Sacral) Chakra

Focus the light of the crystal upon this centre, feel its stimulating energy cleansing it of all emotional overtones. As you do so, firmly instruct the mind of the necessity to develop a sense of detachment in future undertakings, coupled with a dispassionate outlook upon life.

This chakra is linked to the adrenals, small double glands which relate to the 'fight or flight' principles within human nature. Their functions are many and varied, not the least of which is the maintenance of equilibrium within the bodily systems during periods of stress. It produces the hormones adrenalin and cortisone, both of which are vital for different bodily functions.

Adrenalin aids in the elimination of poisons or toxins within the system, whilst cortisone helps to relieve asthma attacks. The stress we all encounter in modern-day life depletes the energy of this gland and this in turn can lead to general listlessness and a great reluctance to face life, particularly situations wherein conflict might ensue.

Flood this chakra with light, stimulating it anew, bringing to the fore all of the positive aspects of one's caring nature, preparing the self in turn for future service-orientated undertakings.

The final centre is that which is termed the Root or Base Chakra, which in turn is linked to the gonads, a gland whose energies are largely devoted to creativity. Situated just above the reproductive organs, this centre relates to the desires of the lower nature which can prove to be troublesome for most of us.

Focus your crystal an inch or two (2–5 cm) away from the Root Chakra and intensify the thought pattern of light, rotating the crystal as you do so. You will soon become aware of the piercing ray projected by the crystal in response to your instruction.

The gonads—the endocrine gland associated with this centre—is primarily involved in the production of thick lymph, sperm and the regulation of sexual activity. Imbalance is revealed in excessive sexual appetites, infertility and mental instability.

Imbalance within the Thyroid and Solar Plexus Chakras is often reflected within the Root Chakra, which may require a good deal of attention. As you become aware of the stimulating energy of the crystal flowing through this centre, rotate the crystal until you

Root Chakra

are absolutely certain that it has returned to its pristine state.

You should by now be conscious of stimulus within all of the chakra centres, each in turn responding to the vitalising inflow of crystalline energy, free of all imbalance or negativity created by mental or emotional stress. Each chakra will now begin to absorb its full quota of those life-sustaining colour rays which permeate the ethers, such activity leading to greater positivity and action.

A word of warning must however be issued here, for having activated all of the spiritual centres in this exercise one is immediately at risk from all of the negative thought forms and emotional debris which the majority of mankind indiscriminately scatters in the ethers day by day. Before leaving the relative safety of one's home environment, create a protective thoughtform to ensure that one may move among the local populace without harm.

There are many recommended methods of closing the chakra centres but that which I personally find to be the most beneficial is the visualisation of a deep blue cloak which should then be wrapped around one from head to feet. For good measure I also close each centre in turn by pulling a symbolic zipper up the cloak towards the Crown Chakra.

10 Developing Mediumistic Qualities

ON holding a rock crystal for the first time, many individuals comment on the fact that they received a sharp jolt in the region of the brow, or that the top of their head is suddenly afire with a tingling energy. This

A natural quartz-crystal ball

unexpected activity is the result of the crystalline forces stimulating the upper spiritual centres, and indeed, a rock crystal can prove to be an invaluable catalyst for all who seriously seek to expand their inner horizons.

From the moment any individual becomes aware of this potent source of spiritual stimulus and consciously utilises a rock crystal within metaphysical practices, a marked acceleration of spiritual momentum occurs, no matter what level of awareness they may have previously attained. Latent intuitive or visionary capacities are swiftly activated, enabling each of these capacities to establish lines of communication with higher planes of consciousness.

Whether aware of the fact or not, we each possess seven senses, five 'outer' or physical senses, and two 'inner' or spiritual senses. The latter—invariably dormant in the majority of mankind—are those which relate to the 'gifts of the spirit', providing one with the ability to 'see' and 'hear' that which transpires on the higher—or finer—levels of consciousness.

The quality of 'insight'—or clairvoyance as it is more readily known—is brought into being through the activation of two 'chakras' or spiritual centres; the Crown Chakra atop the head, and the Brow Chakra, located in the centre of the forehead. Together, these two highly sensitive centres function as the mystical Third Eye.

The secondary quality of 'intuition'—or clairaudience—is brought into operation when the Thyroid or Throat Chakra is activated. A great many individuals unconsciously act upon the silent promptings they receive via this chakra, whilst still more tend to dismiss such inspiration as vain imaginings.

In so doing they ignore valuable guidance and direction which their spiritual mentors endeavour to share

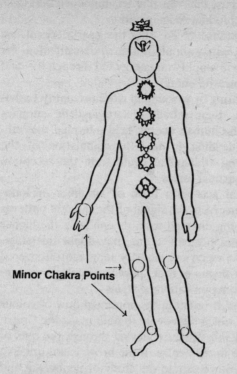

Crown
Brow

Thyroid

Heart

Solar Plexus
Sacral

Root

Minor Chakra Points →

Chakra points

with them. Those who inhabit the higher spiritual planes of consciousness may only communicate with mankind in a telepathic manner, projecting thought patterns which the sensitives among us pick up, either as visual imagery within the Brow Chakra, or intuitively via the Throat Centre.

Conscious reception of intuitive communication becomes comparatively easy once crystalline energies begin to stimulate activity within the Throat Chakra—always provided that the individuals concerned have ceased to dismiss that which enters unbidden into their mind, as the product of imagination.

The importance of the role the quartz crystal can play in such activity should not be underestimated, for rock quartz will amplify all energy fed through it—and thought is powerful energy.

When wearing or working in close proximity to natural crystals, their inbuilt electromagnetic energies react upon the human energy field—termed the 'etheric body'—leading in turn to stimulation of the chakra system, which one could term the reception centres for spiritual forces.

The crystal acts as a form of amplifier or loudspeaker, intensifying the signal of the thought patterns which are being directed towards one from the higher planes of consciousness. Some may doubt this statement, but the electrical industry long ago discovered the ability of slivers of rock quartz to intensify the signals within communications systems.

The task of translating the continual flow of colour and symbols which then begin to pour in via the Crown Chakra, and subsequently viewed through the lens of the inner eye in the centre of the brow, is not quite so simple. It will necessitate the study of symbolism and colour, whilst learning to observe this interchange of visual thought patterns in a totally passive manner.

Should one wish to investigate the field of extrasensory perception—or simply have a desire to attain a greater measure of clarity within communications received from higher dimensions, it becomes necessary to select, with great care, two crystals which will enable one to extend one's spiritual horizons.

As the 'inner' senses relate to the passive or feminine aspect of our dual natures, the greatest priority should be given to the acquisition of a milky or feminine crystal. These are quite difficult to obtain and the

investigator may have to settle for a crystal which has a measure of masculinity or clarity within it.

In selecting suitable crystals for use in the field of mediumistic endeavour, simple guidelines should be followed. Holding a female crystal point upwards in the left hand, adjacent to the Heart Chakra, proceed to project toward it the all-pervading force of unconditional love. Its elemental intelligence will respond by releasing a tingling electromagnetic energy via the point of the crystal. Note the effects of this upon the chakra system. Where this stimulates the Thyroid Chakra, the crystal will prove to be particularly beneficial in intuitive communication, but where its activity is noted upon either the brow or the crown of the head, it is an indication that this is a crystal which will serve to quicken latent visionary capacities.

Within all mediumistic activity, the individual concerned becomes both a receiver and a transmitter and must therefore ensure that their spiritual centres receive a balanced flow of Yin and Yang (positive and negative) energies, whenever communication with unseen forces is being undertaken. This can be achieved by utilising both a masculine and a feminine crystal, and careful selection of a reasonably sized piece of clear quartz will provide that vital counter-balance.

Having located a rock crystal with a masculine energy, which responds joyfully to one's projection of loving thought, it becomes necessary to first dedicate both crystals to Universal Purpose and then to programme each in turn for the specific task they are to fulfill.

A simple visualisation technique will enable one to achieve this goal. Create a mental image of a blackboard, upon which the words 'store memory of visions' clearly appear, and project this within the female crystal, adding the words 'when I instruct, store memory of clairvoyant vision and intuitive direction'. The next step is to take the male crystal and to programme this with a suitable mental instruction: 'Release your power. Activate my chakras'. If so desired, this instruction can be amended so that it relates only to the three upper chakras, thus ensuring a flow of Yin and Yang energies within those centres during periods of communication.

With both crystals duly programmed, they will now follow one's instructions at any given time, provided that they are first re-activated with loving thoughts, followed swiftly by the words of command. The male crystal should then be placed on the floor between the feet, with its faceted point directed inward, where it

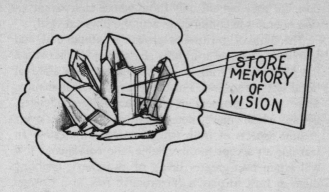

will release its energies into one's Etheric Field. These in turn will be directed towards their specific target by the memory pattern within the crystal. The feminine crystal is always held in the left hand, point upward, adjacent to the Heart Chakra, from which position it will act as a transformer of all incoming thought patterns.

At first, little but the energy interchange will be noted by the investigator, but day by day, one's level of sensitivity will begin to increase, until at last, moving points of light and colour will become clearly visible where development of the visionary capacities is taking place; or in the receipt of clear thought patterns, where the focus of attention is upon the inner ear.

A point little understood by the majority of those who seek to activate clairvoyant faculties is that not all sensitives will 'see' with their physical eyes open. Indeed, the great majority of mediums may only 'perceive' or 'sense' the non-physical dimensions when their physical eyes are closed. It becomes necessary for all to ascertain for themselves the precise manner in which their capacities function. For this reason I do *not* recommend a crystal ball to all would-be visionaries, despite their long association with the field of divination, for they benefit only those whose clairvoyant vision operates in conjunction with the physical sight.

The spiral of spiritual outgrowth is without end, and few among us may truthfully claim to have discovered the fountain of truth or to have attained a state of 'total-self' awareness. For the great mass of humanity, there is the prospect of many daunting challenges, within which one's determination to locate ever-greater aspects of truth will be continually tested. In learning to accept the inevitable, the courageous few will attain ever-greater levels of awareness, enabling them in turn to play a constructive role in a Cosmic Scenario designed to quicken spiritual consciousness within the entire human race.

The extraordinary ability of quartz crystals to bring about a quickening of spiritual sensitivity is highlighted within an unusual experience undergone in a large European museum a year or so ago.

A group of friends took me to view their national treasures, which included many rare and beautiful jewelled pieces, gathered over many centuries. My contemplation of these was interrupted by one young friend to whom I had given a rock crystal the previous day. 'Can you explain why I should receive an electric shock every time I approach the jewel cases with my crystal?' queried this rather perplexed young man.

As I had not provided him with any information on the properties or abilities of rock crystals, he had been using it rather in the manner of a touchstone, and I realised that he had inadvertently stumbled upon a use for crystals which I had not previously considered. Deciding that this was a field worthy of investigation, we arranged to return in two days suitably armed with rock crystals.

Upon our return to the museum, I gave a crystal to each of them, asking. 'Can anyone feel any sensation or tingling energy?' There was a mystified shaking of heads. Under the ever-watchful gaze of several guards (who obviously recognised us from our earlier visit), we approached the different exhibits to test out the powers of our crystals.

Without exception, the rock crystals acted as keys to the vast storehouse of memory locked within the many jewelled pieces displayed there. This in itself had been created centuries earlier, forged from the emotions of their former owners. Many of the vibrations we encountered that day were far from pleasant.

The overall experience served to illustrate to my companions the power of emotionally charged thought patterns. It has long been known that every item of personal clothing or jewellery will absorb the magnetic vibrations of its wearer, but due to their crystalline structure, gems retain those vibrations with clarity not encountered in more porous materials. When one utilises a quartz crystal in the manner described, one calls upon the combined resources of the entire Mineral Kingdom, which in turn will amplify all memory patterns stored within such items.

During the remainder of that afternoon, my companions and I experimented with every rare and precious object within that building, experiencing a number of extremely unpleasant vibrations during the course of the afternoon, particularly from a large ivory figure which had previously belonged to Louis IV. I myself had to retreat in a state of disorientation from a large aquamarine piece which I had greatly admired, without ill effect, upon my earlier visit. This exercise brought home to me the forewarning that those of a Leo disposition should avoid aquamarine, a negative gemstone for them, a point I had not, until that day, fully accepted.

For those possessed of an adventurous spirit, I would recommend similar forms of experimentation, utilising rock crystals as divining rods, *providing* that one has fully adapted to their energies or become sensitive to the vibrations they emit. In a similar manner, quartz can be used to dowse for power points upon maps; to test the energy levels or vibrations within other objects; or to protect oneself from negative thought forms emanating from an outer source.

11   Meditation

THIS particular form of self discipline is all too often sidestepped by those with a Western upbringing, for the pattern of lifestyle experienced within our hemisphere does not readily lend itself to such pursuits, but for those who are prepared to follow this pathway towards Self Realisation, it can often produce the most gratifying results.

The initial hurdle—which so very often defeats those who seek out the inner path—is that of attaining a measure of mental clarity. In such cases the mind is all too often filled to overflowing with mental refuse arising from tendencies to worry over inconsequentials. Whenever such an individual seeks to establish a period of mental silence, a multitude of non-related thought patterns vie for attention, thus preventing the establishment of inner harmony.

Assistance in some form or other then becomes necessary if the student is to overcome this major obstacle. What better aid than a rock crystal—whose major benefits are known to take place upon mental levels?

Select a clear, masculine crystal—its clarity representing the state of mind desired by the student—hold this in the left hand, point uppermost, and commence to project a loving thought pattern towards its elemental inhabitant. As it in turn joyfully responds by releasing the stimulating electromagnetic energy of the crystal, proceed to dedicate it to Universal Purpose.

Finally, one must programme the crystal in such a manner that it will serve not only to stimulate activity within the chakras, thereby focusing mental energies upon the contemplative pattern, but also to act as a recording instrument.

Rock crystals have the capacity to perform somewhat like a video recorder, storing memory of whatever vision or inspiration one receives during the meditative state; but quite naturally, they may carry only one programme at any given time. I would therefore suggest the use of simple imagery and/or commands to achieve one's goal.

A mental image of a video recorder could perhaps be considered or visualise a blackboard upon which the instruction 'record all meditation patterns' is clearly written. Such a programme must be re-activated before any subsequent exercise by the projection of a thought pattern of 'love', coupled with the command 'record meditation patterns from this point on'.

Whatever imagery the crystal captures during these exercises will be stored within its structure until one commands the elemental 'replay all recorded patterns'.

However, some among you may find that, despite following such instructions, they are quite unable to still their mental activity, with the result that no meaningful vision or form of communication can be established. In cases like these, it would be as well to consider some basic exercises as a preliminary to meditation.

Deep-breathing exercises are known to aid the attainment of states of mental clarity and I therefore

suggest that all who experience difficulty with meditation should practise such exercises. At the outset,
these can proceed at one's own rhythm, but to ensure
that unwanted thought patterns do not continue to dis-
turb the period of contemplation, one must learn to
focus the mind upon a definite breathing pattern. The
first step is to breathe in slowly to the count of 6, filling
one's lungs with oxygen. Hold the breath to the count
of 6 and then slowly begin to exhale, again to the
count of 6. You may find this particular rhythm difficult to sustain; if you do, a little experimentation with
various rhythms will enable you to locate a breathing
pattern which is comfortable.

Once established, rhythmic breathing becomes a
natural adjunct to all meditation exercises and ensures

a greater measure of success, for the mind is unable to focus upon distracting situations while it is firmly focused on the need to maintain the rhythm of the breathing pattern.

The second step is to attempt to visualise a simple representation of light, either as a ray of the purest light entering the mind, a candle flame, or the sun. For those of you who experience difficulties with visualisation techniques, I suggest holding a thought pattern of 'light' within the mind, for this will produce the same results—always remembering to maintain the breathing pattern. As one breathes in—draw that light within the self, feel it penetrating every cell and atom of your body—now hold that light deep within the self before slowly exhaling, sharing that light with all of Creation as you do so. The benefits which arise from this particular exercise will very soon become apparent.

During meditation, the eyes should remain firmly closed to ensure that one is not distracted by disturbing factors within the immediate vicinity; all too often the temptation to break the meditative pattern is too great, for, having become aware of a source of light around and about them, some people feel an overwhelming desire to ascertain that it does not originate in an external source, and their joy when they discover that it does not is tempered with awareness that they have temporarily lost touch with that source of enlightenment.

The student has now established a bridgehead and may now proceed to attempt other forms of visualisation. For meditation practices to be truly effective, they should be undertaken at precisely the same time each and every day. In so doing students consciously re-align themselves with the rhythm of the Universe. It is only when we discover this truth and determine to adjust our time schedules accordingly that real progress is made.

All too often 'time' is regarded and measured through patterns established by mankind to indicate the passage of the human race through this world of matter; this sort of 'time' is illusionary. For those who are prepared to 'tune-in' to the universal rhythm each day, untold benefits will result as Beings of Light attune to their unspoken need and in turn seek to answer this in a telepathic manner.

Throughout this book I continually refer to the elemental inhabitants of all rock crystals. Many ask me, 'What exactly is an elemental—what do they look like?' Quite simply, the elemental is an energy without form. However, the elemental within your crystal will take on whatever form you consciously—or subconsciously—believe it to possess. It may therefore appear to you as a bright and shimmering energy, rather like that of a filament within an electric bulb. For others it may take on the form of an elf, or a dwarf, even that of an angel, for thought is creative and the crystal merely reflects back to us the thought form we have released into the ethers.

One further point of view which is worthy of discussion relates to the level of evolution so far attained by the life-force which inhabits the Mineral Kingdom. Mankind tends to take a lofty overview, feeling that as we have attained a measure of self-will and self control, we are the monarchs of this particular plane of matter, and all else is subject to our will.

While this is correct in part, it is not necessarily a point of view shared by the elementals themselves, who are fully aware of their divine origin and respond with some amusement to our assumption that ours is the highest level of attainment.

In common with all life-forms that currently inhabit

this plane of matter, the elementals within the Mineral Kingdom are poised on the brink of change. This will necessitate their breaking free of their current crystalline forms in order that they might eventually locate expression within the second Kingdom on this plane of matter, the Vegetable (or Plant) Kingdom. To achieve this end, they will require a great deal of assistance from mankind, who in turn must be prepared for an expansion of consciousness in the not-too-distant future.

Let me now complete this chapter by sharing with you a very simple visualisation technique, whereby you might encounter the indwelling elemental of your particular crystal.

Sitting in a comfortable position, commence your rhythmic breathing pattern, holding the crystal within your left hand, point uppermost. As the breathing pattern begins to establish a feeling of tranquility within the self, visualise your crystal changing from solid matter to a more fluid form, capable of expansion. Slowly, the uppermost facet will open before you, enabling you in turn to enter therein.

Stop and take stock of your surroundings. The air should feel cool, clear and crisp, the atmosphere alive with an unseen energy. Gaze upward towards the uppermost facets of the crystal and note the flow of colour which eventuates from the inflow of light. Observe this as it flows around the crystal, eventually surrounding you with every hue of the rainbow. Draw this vitalising energy within the self, feeling its healing force removing all states of disharmony. Stay with this cleansing force until you feel totally refreshed and renewed. It may take some time.

Within the flow of colour you should now be able to perceive a crystalline stairway, twisting and winding its way towards the upper portion of the crystal. Begin to ascend, slowly, climbing into a rarified atmosphere, wherein the energy noted earlier becomes more intense. Once at the top of the stairway you will become aware of a previously unnoticed level or platform, upon which is seated the elemental. It may be somewhat nervous, your unexpected invasion of its domain causing it some alarm—so project love towards it, thereby stilling its fear of you.

Take note of its form and await its response to your loving thoughts. (This is almost certain to be an instantaneous acceptance of your right to be there.) Now approach, and in thought, begin to establish a relationship. Advise the elemental of your requirements; of the purpose for which you acquired the crystal—and of the level of assistance you will now require from the elemental itself. Above all, become familiar with this, your younger brother or sister, and seek to ascertain just what you in turn might do to assist the elemental to achieve its own necessary pattern of outgrowth.

When you feel that you have established a harmonious relationship, and possess a measure of understanding of the needs of the elemental, take your leave of it for the present and begin to descend that spiral stairway, entering once more into the flow of colour within the body of the crystal.

Once again, absorb this stimulating force, drawing it into every cell within your body, renewing physical energy levels as you do so. Look around your crystal once more, noting all salient points before departing in the same manner in which you entered the crystal.

Slowly restore the crystal to its original solid form within your hand and return to the conscious state. Where you wish to review the entire experience, re-

quest the elemental to replay all meditative patterns
recorded, switch the crystal to your right hand, and
relive your recent experience.

This exercise may be repeated as frequently as desired, but should one wish only to restore low energy
levels, simply enter into that glorious flow of colour
within the body of the crystal. One may then utilise the
crystal as a stimulus within many similar meditative
patterns, acquiring new insights and awareness as one
does so. The overall purpose behind the life experience is to acquire a measure of growth, an expansion
of one's level of awareness, and the repayment of a
measure of those debts we have all accrued during earlier physical embodiments. The use of the rock crystal
in such exercises enables one to achieve two-thirds of
this goal.

12   Etheric Stimulation

THROUGHOUT this book, I have endeavoured to illustrate different methods of increasing one's spiritual momentum using rock crystals. But, as yet, I have not

Lizard and energy field—Kirlian photography (repro-duced courtesy Gunter Leeb)

touched upon the subject closest to my heart, one which is perhaps of primary importance to all of mankind—the restoration of health and well-being.

Some years ago, a North American doctor asked me to co-operate in treating some of the recipients of his treatment whose health conditions were not responding to established forms of treatment. Within his clinic, each room was equipped with a large cluster of quartz crystals, and all natural healing treatments I undertook within the vicinity of those formations were so powerful and the results so astounding, that I began research into this intriguing phenomenon, the results of which I share here.

Rock quartz crystals are geometric structures that are naturally aligned with the earth's magnetic fields. The energy they attract to themselves from such fields, coupled with their own inbuilt electromagnetic force, provides a powerful form of stimulus, extremely beneficial to anyone who is physically depleted.

When this vitalising force is consciously introduced into the Etheric Body, or electromagnetic field of any individual, it results in an almost instantaneous restoration of bodily energy. Rock crystals therefore provide a powerful healing force, one which all therapists involved in the natural healing field are recommended to experiment with.

Rock quartz has long been known to produce a natural harmony between mankind and the electromagnetic energies which continually flow through the ethers. These in turn aid the formation of the positive and negative ions, so essential to the continued well-being of mankind.

Those who feel lethargic or listless, who lack vitality and are constantly weary, anyone who has undergone surgery in recent years, are all individuals who will gain great benefit from treatment with rock crystals.

All have one thing in common: their health conditions are linked to a break in their outer energy field, that which is termed the Etheric Body.

All life forms currently in existence on this planet possess a similar energy field, a truth long known to students of esoterica, but which has only become common knowledge with the advent of Kirlian photography. This high-speed electrical process reveals both the vitality within the leaf and lizard illustrated, together with its corresponding electromagnetic field. Note that when the leaf was re-photographed some hours later, it revealed a marked decline in its overall energy, much

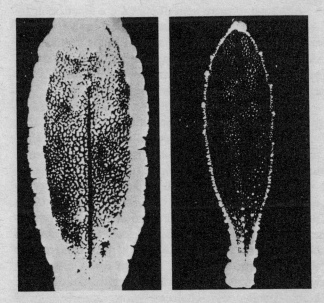

A leaf and its energy field   The same leaf several hours later

Kirlian photograph (reproduced courtesy Gunter Leeb)

as the human form does when there is a breakdown in
its energy supply.

Whenever we abuse the physical body through
over-indulgence in negative thought patterns, such as
habitual worrying or fear, we place great stress upon
the glandular system, which in turn is unable to maintain a natural rhythm within the bodily cycles. Where
we consume large quantities of those foods that are
deficient in vital nutrients, or fail to provide the body
with sufficient rest or sleep, the eventual result is a
breakdown within our natural defence mechanism,
leading in turn to all manner of 'dis-ease' or imbalance.

Although modern anaesthetics are a great boon for
those undergoing painful surgery, they are not without
their side-effects, and are said by some medical authorities in the United Kingdom to have an adverse
effect upon certain parts of the body, particularly the
eyes. Indeed, some surgeons now advise people
undergoing treatment to allow a period of some two
years to elapse before consulting an optician, thus
allowing the eyesight to revert to its normal level—
premature prescribing of stronger lenses can result
in an unnecessary weakening of the eyesight.

Wherever the physical form has undergone operative surgery, there will be a corresponding break within
the outer Etheric Body. Cartilage operations, abdomi-
nal surgery and habitual worrying, all result in the loss
of vitalising electromagnetic energy. Accidents, such as
a broken arm, leg or toe, can also result in a break
within the energy field in the vicinity of the damaged
limb, causing the vitalising force absorbed from
health-giving foods and restful sleep to be dissipated,
leading in turn to general debility. Unlike many health
disorders, such breaks within this outer body are not
rectified by the passage of time, as I discovered when

seeking to assist a man of mature years who persistently complained of lethargy and general weariness. A check on his energy field revealed gaps in the vicinity of both knees, areas where, he later informed me, he had received bullet wounds during World War 2.

Damage to the outer energy field can be repaired by a healing therapist, utilising a number of rock crystals. The individual concerned should be placed upon a table and a clear, masculine crystal positioned point downward an inch or two (3–5 cm) above the crown of the head. Between the feet, point inwards, place a feminine or milky crystal, to affect a balance of Yin

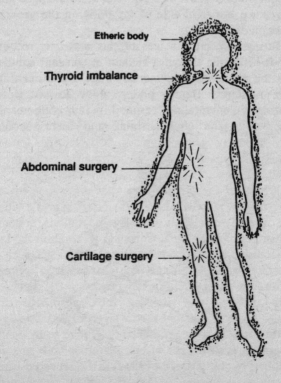

and Yang energies, and finally, within each hand, site a small crystal, to ensure an equal flow of energy to all parts of the body. That in the left hand should be placed with its faceted tip directed towards the head, and that in the right hand with its natural point aligned with the feet. Where possible, the crystals within the hands should also be masculine and feminine, the former placed in the right hand, the latter in the left.

Select a fifth crystal—one that has previously been programmed to indicate imbalance within the energy field and which is light enough to respond to the slightest indication of imbalance—and, with a slow circular motion, move this crystal around the head and then down the right side of the body, in the general direction of the feet.

During the initial stages of this act, it is recommended that the therapist remain in constant contact with the elemental intelligence of the crystal, continually projecting a thought pattern of love towards it. In return the elemental will respond by indicating imbalance within the physical body and corresponding

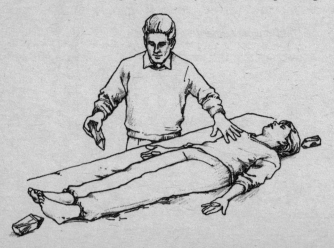

breaks in the Etheric Form. This it achieves by simply refusing to move from the points so indicated.

In turn, the therapist will experience the disharmony in one of several ways, depending on their level of sensitivity. Some may note this as a sensation of heat in those areas where the crystal ceases its motion, for magnetic energies tend to be cool and imbalance in such fields will be experienced as warmth. Others may sense a powerful outflow of tingling energy from the crystal at such points, while the clairvoyants among you will note any breakdown within the energy field as star-like bursts of glowing light.

Wherever the crystal ceases its motion, the therapist should intensify the thought pattern of 'love', and, adding to it one of 'light', project both through the crystal towards the indicated point of imbalance. This will result in an intensification of the flow of electromagnetic energy from the crystal, which in due course will indicate the restoration of harmony by continuing its onward movement. The therapist should note the points of stress so indicated and discuss these with the individual concerned upon completion of the treatment.

Having thoroughly checked the right side of their body, continue the therapy by moving slowly up their

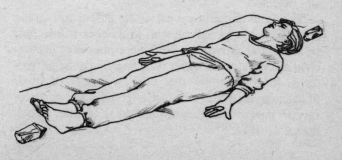

left side, slowly rotating the crystal as you do so, until one again reaches the crown of the head, carefully noting any further points of stress on the way. Once this has been accomplished the recipient should then be requested to lie face downwards in order that the process may be repeated on the back, for one often encounters much stress in the spinal region.

The final segment of this therapy requires the person concerned to relax in a prone position for a further 10 minutes, permitting the quartz crystals to complete the act of re-energising his or her Etheric Body. It is during this final phase of the treatment that most individuals become sensitive to the inflow of the electromagnetic energy, often complaining of pressure in certain regions of the body.

In all, this treatment may take some 20 minutes to complete, following which the recipient may feel slightly disorientated. The therapist should now remove the crystals and encourage the recipient to remain in the relaxed position while relating that which they have experienced. Invariably they will report sensations of almost unbearable heat, particularly in areas where the crystalline energies were specifically focused. Further probing may well reveal the existence of long-standing health problems centered within those areas of the body where a break within the energy field was detected.

This form of therapy is extremely potent and should be sufficient to permit all who experience it to return to a full and active life, but where poor diet, insufficient exercise or indulgence in negative thought patterns form part of the original cause of their imbalance, instructive counselling will also be necessary to ensure that they do not create further imbalance.

For many who read these words, it may not always be possible to locate a suitable crystal therapist, but the great beauty of such treatment lies in its very simplicity, for it may be undertaken by any individual who is prepared to co-operate with the unseen elemental forces. Indeed, those who suffer from exhaustion due, say, to influenza or post-operative shock, can gain great physical stimulus from the electromagnetic energies emanating from rock quartz.

Lying flat on the floor—or on the bed—place the crystals in position: the clear or masculine crystal point downwards in the region of the crown of the head, the feminine or milky quartz situated at the feet, faceted tip inwards. Small crystals should also be placed in the palms of each hand, that in the left hand pointed at the head, and that in the right, pointed towards the feet.

It is essential to project a thought pattern of 'love' towards each crystal in turn throughout the exercise in order to obtain the desired results. And, if gentle music can be played for the duration of this exercise, it will result in the release of a more intense form of energy from all of the crystals.

Ten to 15 minutes of such stimulation will normally prove to be quite sufficient to restore the equilibrium of even the most exhausted of individuals, but in cases where the person concerned has recently undergone surgery, still greater benefits would accrue if one crystal were to be focused for a further 5 minutes on that portion of the anatomy. This should be held an inch or two (3–5 cm) above the body, again focusing a thought pattern of light through the crystal. Such an act will aid the restoration of the energy field at that point and prevent further depletion.

Despite being able to visibly demonstrate the stimulating effect of rock quartz on physically depleted individuals, there are still a great many observers who remain unconvinced, retaining a healthy scepticism of such acts. Being largely practical by nature, they demand an uncomplicated explanation of the mechanics of crystal therapy.

There are a number of reasons why rock quartz is so effective in treating debilitating health conditions, but primarily it is due to the interchange of energy affected by the thought patterns of the therapist.

The projection of loving thought penetrates the physical mass of the mineral substance, activating the indwelling energy force—which I have called the 'elemental'. The subsequent release of the electromagnetic energy of that crystalline structure, coupled with the magnified force of love, result in a powerful stimulation of the human energy field, known as the Etheric Body. This interchange of energy restores depleted vitality, bringing about a general feeling of well-being.

Rock quartz formations have an amazing effect on the fluids of the human body, which in themselves in some ways resemble crystalline structures. The crystal therapist who sensitises the minor chakras of their hands prior to the healing act by placing them within the energy field generated by a large formation of rock quartz, can, in turn, greatly influence the bodily fluids of the person undergoing treatment. This is particularly noticeable where the individual concerned is subject to water retention, for treatment with quartz crystals can stimulate a malfunctioning glandular system, thereby aiding the natural elimination of excess fluids.

This point was particularly demonstrated in a North American clinic some years ago when I was asked to assist a young woman suffering from multiple sclerosis. In great fear of total immobility, this young lady was undergoing several forms of treatment, when her doctor suggested that a course of natural healing therapy might produce a breakthrough. Her major health problem was accompanied by a severe malfunction of the thyroid gland, no doubt aggravated by fear. This had created a state of imbalance within her bodily system, causing her to retain fluid to an alarming degree. Without warning, her body would balloon until she appeared to be in an advanced stage of pregnancy, causing her further despondency, particularly as she was a single woman.

The first encounter proved to be a learning experience for us both. Acting on impulse, I decided to place

my hands above a large quartz formation sited close
by, experiencing the tingling energy for several mo-
ments before undertaking the healing act. Once this
had commenced, my concentration was soon disturbed
by cries of alarm from the woman concerned. Somewhat apprehensive as to what I was about to discover,
I opened my eyes to find that as my hands moved over
her 'outer' or 'etheric' body, the fluids in her greatly
distended stomach rose and fell in a manner resem-
bling the ebb and flow of the tide.

I later discovered that the act of charging my own
energy field within that of the quartz formation had
transformed my hands into large magnets, which in
turn affected the bodily fluids of this young woman,
moving them at will. An even greater discovery lay
ahead of me once she turned over to enable me to
work on her spine.

Once again my concentration was broken, this time
as I became consciously aware of a soft, pliable substance within my hands, which I was busily stretching
along the spinal column. Feeling certain that my hands
had somehow become entangled in some item of the
young woman's underclothing, I opened my eyes in
some trepidation. However, nothing was amiss on the
physical level. My hands remained—as they were intended to remain—some inches above her physical
body, working with her electromagnetic field. For a
brief moment in time, the substance of that energy
field had become temporarily three-dimensional, enabling me to make due corrections therein.

I must state that I endeavoured to assist this young
woman on many occasions following this initial treatment, but always within the privacy of my own apart-
ment. None of these manifestations were ever

repeated, due no doubt to the fact that I was unable to use the energy field of that particular quartz formation at the clinic.

◇◇◇◇◇◇◇◇◇◇◇◇◇◇◇◇◇◇◇◇◇◇◇◇◇◇

13 Healing Mind, Body and Spirit

THE pace of modern life is currently placing a great deal of stress on mankind, particularly mental stress, and in ever-growing numbers those around us are falling prey to disorders spawned by our technological society. If that which we have created is not to destroy mankind, then those who have sought to serve others in the field of natural healing must begin to adapt, expanding their horizons to accommodate some of the new technology within their healing treatments.

For many natural healers this may prove to be a difficult hurdle to clear, for the practice of 'laying-on-of-hands' has served them well in the past. They must, however, come to terms with the fact that the physical problems they endeavour to treat have often had their origin within the mind of those concerned, and that the effects of negative thoughts are first reflected in the outer etheric form. Restoration of harmony within mind, body and spirit must therefore commence with the cleansing of this outer energy field.

Playing a large part in the electronic age is the 'humble' rock crystal, this being due to its ability to store memory and to amplify energy which is fed through it. Throughout time, mankind has used this simple mineral structure in sacred ceremonies to affect the restoration of balance in the physically afflicted, and those healing practitioners who desire to form part of the vanguard for the New Age must seriously consider this ancient form of therapy.

There is, of course, a great deal of scepticism with regard to the stated abilities of rock quartz, for we are all conditioned by the society within which we have our being. Knowledge of the ability of minerals and gemstones to affect changes in health patterns was suppressed by early Christian leaders, who sought to reduce the influence of pagan beliefs. As most gems at that time were engraved with the symbols of those

A storage crystal with inclusions

faiths and handed down from generation to generation, one can see the logic behind such activity.

But a New Age dawns; the intelligence within the
Mineral Kingdom must now seek to acquire awareness
of this 'outer' world and this may only be accomplished
with the full assistance of mankind.

Developing an understanding of the different abilities of the many crystalline forms is of primary importance for the natural healer, who will be expected to
assist with the transmuting of many forms of imbalance
during the course of their careers. As no two crystals
will react in precisely the same manner, experimentation is the order of the day.

Some quartz formations have areas of cloudiness
within their make-up, serving to confuse the unini-
tiated who incorrectly assume that this gives the crystal
a feminine quality. To their chagrin, the quartz invariably clears once it has been utilised in healing therapies, for that cloudiness is invariably moisture trapped
within the quartz structure. Where there are inclusions, such as slivers of tourmaline within a crystal, it
can prove to have extremely potent energies and
should be handled with care, for tourmaline's unusual
electrical properties are well-known.

The variety preferred by the majority of crystal
therapists is the clear, unsullied quartz which is mined
in Arkansas in the United States, which, due to its
clarity, emits extremely powerful energies. These in
turn will stimulate mental and/or physical activity
within all who are exposed to their vibration, providing a plus factor for those who suffer from physical
debility, lethargy, or stress-related disorders.

Some individuals, however, develop health conditions which arise from over-stimulation, such as nervous tension or migraine attacks. In seeking to treat
such stress-related conditions, the therapist should se-

lect a large feminine or milky quartz, whose calming
energies will swiftly counteract the effects of over-
stimulation. Holding the quartz in the right hand, several inches above the crown of the head, project a
thought pattern of 'peace' through the crystal towards
the person concerned while placing the left hand in the
region of the Thyroid Chakra. This combination of
thought and crystal power, coupled with the balancing
of the flow of energy through this most sensitive of

A masculine crystal

centres, will bring relief in a matter of minutes. Indeed, I advocate attunement with the chakra system of
the recipient throughout a crystal treatment, for I have
discovered that such activity greatly increases the
overall benefits arising from such therapy.

When a natural healer acts as a receiver, transformer and transmitter for the Healing force, the resultant outflow of power is readily identifiable as a tingling force flowing from the hands. However, when a quartz crystal is introduced into the healing act, the crystal becomes the focal point for the healing forces, leading to a loss of sensation by the human channel. During the initial stages of acclimatisation to quartz crystal, this lack of sensation becomes a source of some concern for the natural healer, who may be forgiven for wondering if they have now lost their powers. However, the reactions of the recipient to this intensified flow of healing energy should soon put their minds at rest.

In the ancient civilisations, the cleansing of one's Etheric Form of the effects of negative or destructive thought patterns, was considered to be of primary importance. Within their vast healing temples, the priests subjected the individual concerned to the potent forces emanating from large quartz formations. These in turn, due to their extremely high rate of vibration, transmuted the negativity within the Etheric Form, restoring this to its original clarity. Until this had been achieved, no other form of treatment was undertaken.

Following the withdrawal of knowledge about the use of crystalline forces, these practices fell into disuse and the subsequent suppression of awareness relating to the occult properties of gemstones, coupled with the development of modern medicine, has focused the majority of attention on the physical form. Today, great emphasis is placed upon the need to prevent further suffering and far too little to locating and eradicating the original, long-forgotten cause.

Those seeking to re-acquaint themselves with crystal therapy will need to acquire a minimum of four crystals, two of medium size and two very small crystals. These should be two masculine and two feminine to ensure a balanced flow of Yin and Yang energies throughout a treatment.

The larger, masculine crystal should always be used as the focal point for the healing energies during treatment, while the larger of the feminine crystals should be placed at the feet of the recipient, with its faceted point inwards. In the left hand of the individual undergoing therapy, place the small, feminine crystal, in order that it might play its part, by directing the revitalising energies up and around the body of the recipient. In the palm of his or her right hand, site the small, masculine crystal with its facets pointed at the feet, to ensure the continuous flow of the electromagnetic energy.

Tests I have conducted reveal that treatments which exclude the quartz crystals from the hands are never quite so effective, for although small, their role is to focus power upon points of imbalance within the central area of the body, aiding the overall return to balance and harmony. On one occasion, when aiding someone suffering from total exhaustion—but who was unable to identify its cause—these smaller crystals swiftly activated a further crystal this individual wore around his neck. This began to pulsate and emit powerful energies which in turn were focused on his thyroid gland. This naturally alarmed him, for until that day, this particular crystal had appeared to be inactive. In this manner the crystals indicated the source of his imbalance in addition to restoring his energy levels.

The left side of the human body is considered to reflect the passive or sensitive aspect of our dual natures, while the right side is stated to represent our active or assertive qualities. Healing energies flow in an ordered rhythm around the body, flowing from left

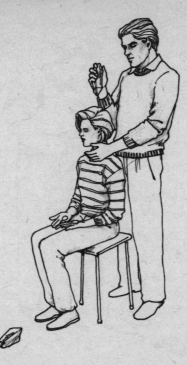

to right, the point of receipt being the physical heart. In natural healing therapies, where the human channel acts as receiver, transformer and transmitter, the left hand is known as the 'power hand', projecting a greater flow of healing force.

However, in crystal therapy, this situation is reversed, with the healing channel becoming just one more link in the cosmic chain of light. The quartz crystal now assumes the role of receiver and transmitter of those healing energies, which it receives from the human channel. To ensure that it plays its role to its fullest extent, the crystal must be held in the right (active) hand.

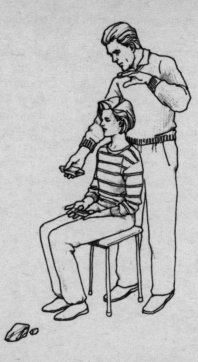

The greatest benefits arising from the use of quartz crystals take place within the Etheric Body and it is upon that outer energy field that crystal therapists should concentrate their attention. Holding the masculine crystal firmly in the right hand, commence the therapy in the region of the Crown Chakra, positioning the quartz 6 or so inches (15–20 cm) above the physical form while placing the left hand adjacent to the Throat Chakra.

The focus of attention on these two very sensitive centres is most important, for together they exert a major influence on the glandular system. As the endocrine glands are highly susceptible to thought patterns the focus of 'love' and 'light' through the quartz crystals brings about stimulus within and without the physical form.

Rotating the crystal slowly over the region of the head, note any points of imbalance and project a thought pattern of 'light' through the quartz towards them. Gradually move towards the right side of the body, rotating the quartz as you do so, moving the left hand now to the region of the Crown Chakra.

As one progresses down the right side of the body of the person concerned, it will soon become necessary to move the left hand to the vicinity of the lower chakra points, to ensure constant attunement to the needs of the recipient. Initially, many students experi-

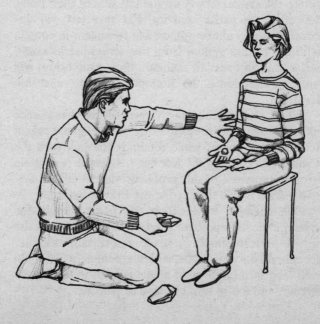

ence a measure of difficulty in focusing upon both the
chakras and the crystal simultaneously, and many seek
to affect an entire treatment with their left hand sited
in the region of the Crown Chakra.

With practice, this use of both hands upon different
areas of the body becomes second nature, its purpose
being to ensure a positive flow of energy throughout
the healing act, while absorbing awareness of the areas
of stress.

For instance, imbalance within the Solar Plexus
Chakra could indicate health problems in the region of
the stomach, with possibly the liver or the gall bladder
requiring attention.

Imbalance will be noted by the therapist as an outflow of heat from the chakra point concerned.

As one reaches the feet of the recipient, begin to
rotate the crystal slowly up the left side of their body,
repeating the earlier activity. The therapist will discover that it is almost impossible to remain in contact
with the chakra system from this somewhat awkward
angle, and in order to maintain their equilibrium will
need to discontinue the attempt until they reach hip
level.

When one reaches the crown of the head once
more, spend some time checking out the spinal region
for points of stress, while retaining the link with the
Crown Chakra with the left hand. Often it is possible
to note potential health problems via the chakra system, which is also reflected in the Etheric Spine.

One example to illustrate this point: should the
crystal indicate a positive reaction in the region of the
thyroid, efforts should be made to ascertain its cause,
for should its origins be within resentment, it could
well lead to a build-up of acidic crystals in the blood-
stream, and this in turn can lead to arthritis.

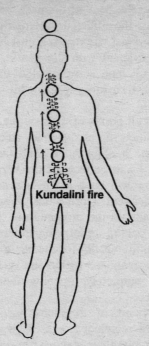

Kundalini fire

The Etheric Spine

Having re-charged the entire energy field of the individual concerned, the therapist should proceed with the next phase of the treatment. Laying aside the crystal, place the left (power) hand upon any area where stress was noted during the cleansing process, ensuring that one maintains the Yin and Yang balance of energies by placing the right hand in an opposite direction.

Where, for instance, a measure of imbalance has been noted in the region of the thyroid, place the left hand in the vicinity of the gland while positioning the right hand on the back of the neck, transmitting healing energy to the afflicted part of the body. At this point the therapist will discover just how valuable the earlier period spent with the quartz crystals has become, for it will have activated all of the minor chakras in the hands, transforming them into highly sensitive instruments.

Deal with all points of disharmony in a methodical manner commencing at the head, freeing the body of stress with the healing touch. This task will be made much easier by the effects of the crystalline energies which by now will have led to a sense of well-being within the recipient. During this phase of the therapy one must maintain the projection of 'love'—this time towards the person undergoing treatment—for it ensures the continuous flow of the healing energies while stimulating a response within the recipient, who will then relax completely, opening themselves to this beneficial force.

When all points of stress have been dealt with, it is the turn of the recipient to express themselves, sharing with the therapist their reactions to the overall experience. This period of sharing is important, serving to affirm that the desired results have taken place, while acting as a teaching point for both participants.

To complete the treatment, the therapist should devote further time to illustrating the power of the mind and how one's negative thought patterns result in states of imbalance. Some instruction on the art of meditation and daily self analysis will further assist the person concerned, helping to prevent future disharmony, as will advice on the need to maintain a healthy and balanced diet, coupled with frequent exercise.

The art of healing must embrace all aspects of the psyche of the individual concerned if it is to remain a viable force for good within the New Age. Those who seek to serve mankind in such a manner must continually seek to expand their mental horizons.

14   Balancing Chakra Energies

IN addition to the information so far shared with regard to healing mind, body and spirit, there remains a further form of treatment which is both powerful and instructive. This involves the use of a crystal pendulum in order to balance the energy flow within the seven spiritual centres of the individual concerned.

Elsewhere in this book I have shown how one may cleanse one's own chakras using a clear quartz crystal. But in situations where a treatment is being undertaken on behalf of others, I strongly recommend the use of a crystal pendulum for several reasons.

First, using a quartz pendulum the therapist will become aware of just which of these spiritual centres reflect imbalance, the information gathered in this segment of the treatment aiding the final act of counselling the individual concerned.

Second, as these are extremely sensitive areas of the body, the use of a large or even medium-sized crystal by a therapist could result in almost unbearable levels of heat or pressure, particularly in the region of the lower chakras. When an individual elects to cleanse their own chakras, it is their thought patterns which

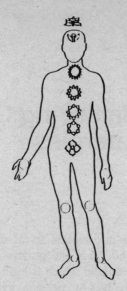

Chakra points

are being fed into those sensitive centres, but when a therapist is involved it is far better to utilise a clear, one-inch (2.5 cm) crystal pendulum which will affect the balancing of energies within these centres without untoward discomfort for the recipient.

There are many conflicting points of view on how such pendulums should be set. Some feel that if one seals the end of a quartz crystal it will no longer be able to absorb energies, and therefore serve no useful purpose. But most pendulums are set in gold or silver, which, like quartz itself, form part of the Mineral Kingdom. While the crystal is still growing in the Earth its base is often rock or sandstone, yet the crystal still absorbs and reflects electromagnetic energies.

Pendulum setting

This point is clearly indicated in the crystal caves maintained in the Far East for initiation purposes. The energies of the Moon are channelled by the surrounding mountains into the caverns where the crystals are located, still embedded within their rock base. In turn these reflect the potent electromagnetic energies, providing a powerful stimulus for those undergoing initiation rites.

Before attempting to balance the energies in the chakra centres, one should first programme the pendulum with specific instructions to ensure that it performs in the desired manner. The different chakra centres have a specific pattern or rhythm, each rotating in an individual manner so it is important that all

therapists understand how these differ in the male and
female forms.

Chakra	Masculine	Feminine
Crown	Clockwise	Anti-clockwise
Brow	Anti-clockwise	Clockwise
Throat	Clockwise	Anti-clockwise
Heart	Anti-clockwise	Clockwise
Solar Plexus	Clockwise	Anti-clockwise
Sacral	Anti-clockwise	Clockwise
Root	Clockwise	Anti-clockwise

Holding the pendulum in the left hand with the faceted point of the crystal pointing upwards, project a
thought pattern of 'love' towards its elemental intelligence. Very soon the effects of this positive vibration
will be reflected in the atoms of your Etheric Form as
an outpouring of energy, usually noted in the region of
the thyroid gland.

You must now programme the crystal in a simple
manner to ensure that it fulfils the desired task. Holding the pendulum by the attached chain, mentally direct the elemental intelligence, 'when I so instruct,
rotate clockwise' while swinging the pendulum in the
required manner, bearing in mind that the elemental
has no knowledge of human terminology. Continue the
programming with 'and when I further instruct, rotate
anti-clockwise', once again swinging the pendulum in
the appropriate direction.

From this point onwards the pendulum will perform
as instructed, although at first it may prove necessary
to project a powerful thought pattern to ensure that
your wishes are obeyed. During the course of a recent
workshop one particular student became quite dis-
traught when, no matter how hard he tried, the pendulum would simply not rotate. Persuading him to

persevere, he eventually discovered a suitable method. 'I've got it!' he cried delightedly. 'I just roll my eyes in the direction I want it to move.' He had discovered that the mental power which directed his eyes to move in such a manner also instructed the elemental of the pendulum.

In addition to the possession of an Etheric Form, we possess several other 'subtle bodies' and the therapist must be prepared at times to operate several inches away from the physical form. We are, after all, but the final link in a great unseen chain of love and light which extends from the God-head, and each of us in turn is directed at all times when we seek to respond to the needs of any individual. There can therefore be no hard and fast rules with regard to such undertakings, merely variable patterns to which we must adapt according to current requirements.

To affect the balancing of the flow of energy within the chakras, first place the individual concerned upon a stool and begin the treatment at the Crown Chakra, for in this manner one will draw the light of the Higher Self down into the lower centres as one descends towards the Root Chakra.

Holding the pendulum on a short length of chain, position it some 2–3 inches (5–8 cm) above the Crown Chakra. If the individual undergoing treatment is of the female gender, instruct the elemental intelligence to rotate anti-clockwise. Initially there may be little response from the pendulum, indeed, it may refuse to move at all. Do not be dismayed, for this is a common reaction—particularly where one has no previous experience of working with pendulums. Renew your efforts, firmly instructing the pendulum to 'rotate anti-clockwise'.

Very slowly it will begin to respond, gathering speed as it does so, often following a wide arc around the

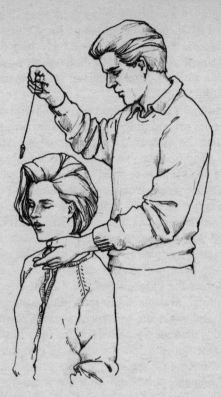

head of the individual concerned. As this is the seat of
the Spiritual Intelligence, one should not be too per-
turbed at such a reaction, but be content to observe
the response of the pendulum as you project a thought
pattern of 'love' towards it. At no time should the
therapist attempt to control the movement of the pendulum, apart from the initial instruction to rotate.
When the energy flow within this centre has been ad-
justed, the pendulum will begin to swing back and
forth before finally coming to a halt.

To facilitate the balancing of the flow of energy within the remaining chakras, the individual concerned should be placed in a prone position on a massage table or healing couch. Once again, position the pendulum some 2–3 inches (5–8 cm) above the centre of the brow and instruct the elemental intelligence, 'rotate clockwise'; once more it will begin to obey your instruction.

The Brow and Crown Chakras form the Inner Eye or Third Eye, that mystical centre which provides in-

sight into higher realms. Where the individual concerned has experienced difficulty in activating this
visionary capacity, they may well be subjected to intense pressure in this region as the pendulum rotates
over the Brow Chakra. In turn, this may be accompanied by a burning sensation deep within the Root
Chakra, such a reaction being an indication of 'lower-
self' opposition to 'higher-self' expression. Where this
occurs the person concerned will need to be counselled
on this point and given instruction on thought control.

Once the pendulum indicates a return to balance by
ceasing its activity, progress towards the Thyroid
Chakra located at the base of the throat. This centre is
often in great need of attention, linked as it is to the
gland which governs metabolism. The therapist should
not be alarmed if the pendulum rotates with great

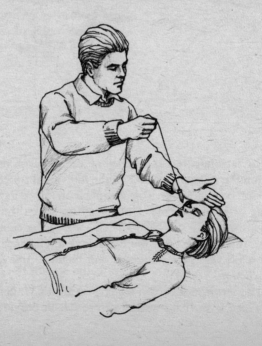

speed at this point. Worry, fear and uncertainty greatly affect the level of activity within this centre, which in turn is linked to the Solar Plexus Chakra, wherein the recipient may now be experiencing a very definite reaction.

The Thyroid Chakra is linked to the intuitive faculty, that which we term our 'sixth sense'. Via this centre we are able to attune to the many telepathic communications which are beamed towards us from the higher Mental Planes. These in turn are intended to aid us to overcome the many self-created hurdles or obstacles we all place on our own path of greater-self awareness. The general tendency to worry or fear— particularly about the unknown—causes imbalance in the thyroid gland which in turn leads to a state of disharmony in the chakra, and blocks the telepathic communication that might have indicated the way ahead.

As the pendulum slows, indicating a return to harmony, move it to the area in the centre of the breast, the Heart Chakra. In the majority of cases, this centre is not operative, possibly due to the fact that the thymus gland to which it is linked begins to atrophy during adolescence.

Should there be no response to your instruction to rotate in a clockwise direction over this centre, the therapist should make a careful note to counsel the person concerned upon the necessity to learn to love others in an unconditional manner if they seriously desire to expand their current level of consciousness.

Where a positive response does occur in this region it may possibly result in a sensation of pressure in the centre of the breast, and in turn may stimulate a tingling sensation within the Sacral Chakra to which it is linked. The Heart Chakra is the seat of the Higher or Spirit Self and is the last of the chakras to be activated, not altogether surprising considering that few among us today can truthfully claim to love others without expectation of return.

The Solar Plexus Chakra is situated just above the navel and is another centre wherein the therapist can expect to encounter a great deal of imbalance, reflected in a wildly swinging pendulum. It is the site of the Lower Will and a point where most of mankind experiences a great deal of tension from time to time.

Instruct the pendulum to rotate in an anti-clockwise direction and intensify the projection of 'love' towards the elemental intelligence, for it will be an unusual occurrence if one is not required to expend a deal of time and effort in restoring harmony to this volatile centre.

As this chakra is concerned with the expression of the Ego or Lower Will, it is closely linked to the Root

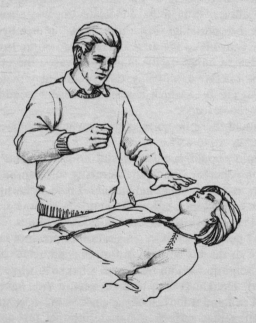

Chakra as well as the thyroid, for all three reflect the responses of our physical natures. As one rotates the pendulum over the solar plexus it may result in a corresponding pressure in the region of the Root Chakra of the individual concerned, which can in turn lead to all manner of misunderstandings. This is one of the reasons why I personally advocate the use of a pendulum, held several inches away from the body when one is undertaking therapy in the region of the chakra points.

Do not be concerned if this centre takes a considerable amount of time to restore harmony. Simply permit the pendulum to accomplish the task you have programmed it for, and when all activity ceases, move on to the sacral centre. This chakra is also known as the spleen centre and is linked to the caring aspect of human nature. Where the individual concerned has a tendency to be emotional, often becoming entangled in the misfortunes of others, this centre may reflect a great deal of imbalance. At the other end of the spectrum one may encounter an individual who is somewhat selfish in their outlook and/or determinedly ambitious. In such cases it is not unusual to receive no response from the pendulum in the region of this chakra.

The final centre is that which is termed the Root or Base Chakra and is located just above the reproductive organs. With some individuals there will be little response from the pendulum when it is focused over this centre, while in others, it will gyrate wildly.

Do bear in mind at all times that the overall purpose of such acts is to balance the flow of energy within all of the various centres in order to ensure that all become equal in their level of activity. It is not the task of a therapist to energise one or more centres

which he or she may mistakenly assume to be out of
balance. The fact that the pendulum gyrates wildly
over some centres and not others does not necessarily
indicate a state of imbalance or over-activity. The therapist must simply be prepared to note the various reactions and to discuss them with the recipient once the
treatment has been completed.

Of all the tasks undertaken in conjunction with rock
quartz, that which utilises a crystal pendulum provides
the most positive and immediate reaction for both
therapist and recipient alike. Indeed, I would strongly
recommend that all who desire to utilise a pendulum in
this manner seek to experience it for themselves on
several occasions before embarking on such therapies.
In this way, given the different moods we are all prone
to, the would-be therapist will have a measure of experience which will aid them in understanding the reactions of others to this extremely potent form of
treatment.

15　Wearing Crystals

As the dissemination of information regarding quartz crystals gathers momentum world-wide, wildly divergent points of view are currently being aired, often by declared leaders in the field. This leads to much confusion among those who are anxious to avail themselves of their many benefits.

Some schools of thought indicate that when a crystal is worn on the person with its faceted point downwards, it will lead to a depletion of physical energies; others say that this is not so. Even greater confusion is created over the manner in which the crystal is set, some indicating that the sealing of a crystal in metal serves to prevent the flow of energy, yet this point is disputed by other specialists who state that the setting has little bearing upon the energy flow.

The answer of course is to follow whatever works best, while experimenting with alternate methods until one discovers that which is correct. A scientist whom I greatly respect, and who has spent a great deal of time and energy studying and testing the various crystalline substances, declares that wearing a quartz crystal with its faceted tip downwards—the manner in which most

quartz crystals are set—does deplete the human energy field.

I largely concur with his findings, with one notable exception. Where any individual is obliged to work in a stressful environment—and given the current pace of life in our modern technological world, the majority among us are—wearing a crystal point downwards over the Heart Chakra will provide a valuable form of protection. The crystal acts as a buffer between the wearer and the source of the stress, absorbing harmful vibrations within its own structure. The moment one leaves that environment the crystal will then resume its normal function, reflecting its energy via its point, depleting the energy field. The answer to this dilemma is either to reverse the faceted point of the crystal so that its energy is directed towards the head, or to remove it.

These statements may appear to be at odds with others made within this book, regarding the benefits which accrue when the energy field of a quartz crystal is brought into close proximity with the body. Such energy, introduced by another individual, does indeed serve to strengthen and re-energise the Etheric Form, but when a quartz crystal is worn within that energy field for any length of time it can produce different results.

To fully appreciate this point one must learn to view the human body as a vast energy field with positive and negative poles. The left side of the body is considered to be feminine, representing the negative pole, and the right side, the masculine or positive pole. The feminine aspect is passive or receptive; the masculine assertive or active.

Energy flows around the body in an ordered and regulated manner from its reception point at the heart, around the body from left to right. A quartz crystal placed in the left hand with its faceted tip directed towards the heart, will introduce a powerful flow of electromagnetic energy which is stimulating to all of the subtle bodies, benefitting the physical form. A crystal placed in the right hand, its tip directed towards the feet, will carry that energy away from the body, leading to depletion, unless a further crystal is sited at the feet, and placed in such a manner as to ensure that the vitalising energy is re-directed into the Etheric Form.

Therefore, select a double-terminated crystal, taking care to set this with a band around its central stem to ensure an equal flow of energy. Such a crystal will stimulate the energy field while serving to protect its wearer from the effects of a stressful environment. Good quality double-terminated crystals of wearable size are difficult to get, but diligent searching should reward the determined. But a word of warning. Such crystals, no matter how small, are generators in their own right, emitting powerful energies that have a cleansing effect upon the emotions of those who wear them. This leads to the release of much-repressed emotion, thereby benefitting their distressed owners,

A double-terminated crystal

for where deep emotions are repressed for any length of time it can lead in the long term to serious illness.

When worn upon the body between the Thyroid and Heart Chakras they serve to activate both of these centres. This will lead to the individual becoming a more loving person and will stimulate any latent intuitive faculty. Once this has been activated, it will forewarn of any impending danger, enabling the wise individual to take avoiding action. The benefits of wearing such a crystal are therefore numerous.

For those who suffer from a weak or impaired memory, a double-terminated crystal can become a great asset, aiding them to store memory of whatever information they gather in the course of their daily lives. They will also prove invaluable to anyone who has at some time undergone electric shock treatment for depression. This somewhat barbaric method of treating the afflicted tends to shatter the Etheric Form and often results in an inability to memorise even the simplest information. Such individuals should wear a double-terminated crystal on the person constantly.

If you wear a crystal all day, it becomes necessary to purify it at night to rid it of all the negative vibrations it has absorbed in the course of your defence. The simplest method is to place it overnight on a cluster of amethyst quartz, for the high rate of vibration of this species will serve to purify the rock quartz of all impurities. Those who choose to ignore this advice will all too soon discover that their crystal has become saturated in negative vibrations and continued use can lead to a general depletion of energies and even to deep depression.

16   Controlling the Kundalini

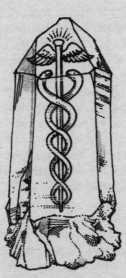

IN their restless search for total awareness, some individuals—ignoring all advice to the contrary—throw caution to the winds and deliberately seek to raise the Kundalini. This symbolic Serpent of Spiritual Fire is

said in esoteric teachings to have its seat at the base of
the spine and to rise through the chakra system, bringing a measure of cosmic consciousness in its wake.

Such an experience—undergone by all would-be
initiates at some point in time—is intended as the ulti-
mate goal of a life spent in the search for truth and
wisdom, during which determined efforts have resulted
in the total mastery of the lower nature.

Sadly, some misguided beings openly invite credu-
lous people in public meetings to attempt to raise the
Kundalini, resulting all too often in disorientation
which can last for several weeks, and in some distress-
ing cases, for years. During this period these unfortunate individuals, who are often highly sensitive and
emotional people, live in a state of great confusion,
subject to the erratic behaviour of this exceptionally
powerful force. In extreme cases the person concerned
can be reduced to a state where he or she, swept by
waves of emotion, cries continuously, to the bewilder-
ment of family and associates.

For those who have not in any measure experienced
this occurrence, it resembles a rushing energy which
thrusts its way upward within the self, rising from the
Root Chakra—seat of the lower nature and base emotions—up to the Thyroid Chakra, the seat of fear in
many individuals, or to the Brow Chakra, the point of
inner vision.

This can lead to a measure of para-normal activity
which can leave an unprepared individual totally be-
wildered and confused. Where they exercise little or
no control over their lower emotions, subsequent involvement in sensual activity will cause the Kundalini
to drop as rapidly as it rose, intensifying their disorientation.

Where the Kundalini has been prematurely activated and the individual concerned is unable or unwilling to adjust to their heightened state of consciousness, it can be countered with the use of a large masculine crystal, suitably programmed by a therapist.

He or she should seek to visualise a caduceus and to project this image within the crystal, coupled with the instruction 'I command you to return to the base of the spine'. The duly programmed crystal should then be placed some 2–3 inches (5–8 cm) away from the Sacral Centre and the command clearly given to the elemental intelligence of the crystal as you begin to focus the full power of your mind on drawing down the serpent of spiritual fire. It may take some 15 minutes or more before the recipient can report a measure of success, and the therapist may be required to repeat this exercise for several days before all returns to normal.

Such an experience is a valuable lesson to those concerned—they will not be so eager to play with Cosmic Fire again. Sadly, it all too often results in the luckless individual forswearing the spiritual path for the remainder of this lifetime, necessitating another embodiment at some future point in time.

17 Psychic Self Defence

SINCE I began my search for truth over 25 years ago, it has been my misfortune from time to time to encounter certain individuals who have sought to control my mind using magic. When one is attacked by hideous thought-forms night after night, one is naturally terrified, particularly if one happens to be sensitive by nature. My automatic reaction during those early days was to switch on every light in the room, and, once calm, to sleep uneasily for the remainder of the night, totally bathed in light.

One evening when such an occurrence took place, I was prevented from taking my usual evasive action by the voice of one of the Spirit Brothers who had by this time begun to play a large part in my life. 'Think of light my Son, project light towards it. Do not switch on your lamp.' This was no easy task. For I readily admit to being quite terrified of the thought-form which stood at the foot of my bed. Reluctantly obeying the command, I began to visualise a ray of pure white light and beamed it towards the malefic force at my bedside. Very slowly it began to retreat before the light and eventually vanished. My lesson here was to first

overcome fear—upon which such thought-forms feed
—and in turn to create a positive counter-thought-
form of light, against which it had no defence.

Some years later, when up against an individual
with powerful mental abilities who was determined to
eradicate every possible light centre in the vicinity, I
discovered that the projection of 'light' was insufficient. To my rescue came the Spirit Brother who suggested 'add love my Son, open up your heart centre
and project pure love—devoid of all condition—in
addition to light.' This was quite a tall order, but in
fulfilling the request I was able to watch in amazement
as the thought-form crumbled before my eyes. 'That
energy has now been transmuted my Son and returns
to its creator who must now deal with it', continued the
Brother, obviously as delighted as I at the results of my
actions.

In such a manner I continued to deal with similar
thought-forms until quite recently when I encountered
yet another power-hungry individual, who used every
trick in the book to break my will. Initially I allowed

fear to colour my judgement, which in turn permitted the thought patterns of this individual to gain entry into my mind, causing ill-health.

Determined not to be overcome by this dark force I requested the aid of the Spirit Brothers—who no longer play such an active role in my life's work. In response I was shown how to use a large cluster of quartz crystals, to help overcome the attacks, all of which came with monotonous regularity just after midnight. 'But first my Son,' counselled the Brother, 'you must forgive this person, for they fear you and they consider their actions to be self-defence.' This admonishment came as something of a surprise, but upon reflection I realised that the Brother's advice was—as always—wise and just.

Placing the selected quartz cluster on the table before me I endeavoured to visualise the person concerned, and then aloud stated 'I forgive you'—projecting love from my Heart Chakra towards them, using the quartz formation to amplify this loving energy. I maintained the projection for some time before switching to a thought-pattern of light, visualising a pure white ray which I also fed into the crystal.

I might add that this was not an easy task to accomplish, for the human aspect of my nature still held a measure of resentment, and the recipient of my attempts at brotherly love was obviously none too happy either, for the attacks resumed with great ferocity. However, as I now slept with a suitably programmed feminine crystal beneath my pillow, I came to no further harm and could even laugh at the situation. Each day I renewed my focus of love and light through the crystal formation until the attacks finally ceased.

One further point is worthy of mention, for it may assist those who may be unfortunate enough to cross the local representative of the dark forces. Whilst still undergoing attack I was given warning (while in the meditative state) that I required greater protection and that I should that day carry with me a large amethyst cluster, in addition to the very large quartz formation. As the combined weight of both items was somewhere in the region of 7 kilograms I was not exactly overjoyed at the prospect. 'Why is that necessary?' I queried. 'For purification,' was the somewhat cryptic reply. Fortunately I was sensible enough to heed the warning and very soon discovered that I had become the victim of yet another attack, with a large circle of salt spread over my workplace.

The Brothers then advised me to sweep this away and to sprinkle the entire area with water before placing both the amethyst cluster and the quartz formation within the area where this misguided individual had sought to trap me. I then invoked light from the higher mental planes and from the Ascended Masters also and was rewarded by the most intense ray of the purest light descending into the area. This was then absorbed within the structure of both crystalline forms which in turn began to radiate that light, thereby protecting me from further harm.

For those of my readers who are unfortunate enough to come under psychic attack I suggest that you endeavor to procure a very large cluster of quartz crystals and a large milky (feminine) crystal. The latter should be very carefully programmed to protect and placed beneath the pillow upon retiring for the night. (Such attacks invariably come during the hours of darkness.)

It is then very important to forgive the individual concerned, never for one minute allowing fear to enter your mind, and then to utilise the large quartz cluster as a generator of light and love. Visualise a ray of rose

A feminine crystal

pink light issuing from your Heart Chakra, for this is
the colour which represents Christ Consciousness and
unconditional love, and project it towards your antag-
onist via the cluster, coupled with a ray of pure white
light. Provided that one undertakes this act with full
determination each and every day, seeking to return
negativity with positive and constructive thought patterns, you will emerge the victor in such confronta-
tions.

To conclude this chapter, the following may provide
food for thought. I discovered some weeks after the
cessation of the attacks that I had subconsciously desired to undergo this unpleasant experience, and had
requested it in order that I might gather valuable information from the encounter. It was yet another of

those hair-raising situations which it has been my misfortune to undergo in recent years, wherein the Higher (Spirit) Self acted without the conscious consent of the Lower (Physical) Form.

18 Healing Animals

THE various members of the Animal Kingdom demonstrate a particular instinct or sixth sense, which leads them to eat certain herbs or grasses in order to correct minor physical disorders, and this characteristic is clearly evidenced in household pets. During my many years of service in the field of natural healing I have been continually astounded at the ability of animals to recognise healing energies, which they respond to in the most amazing manner. It would appear that they are also capable of recognising the various rates of vibration within the Mineral Kingdom.

Friends who possess two dogs, one an Irish setter, the other a black German shepherd, were concerned about the health of both pets. The setter had developed a form of skin cancer which would not respond to natural forms of treatment; the German shepherd was extremely listless and flea-ridden.

Somewhat reluctantly they were persuaded to permit the veterinarian to operate on the skin cancer of the setter, but as the weeks passed, the wound refused to heal, causing them great concern for they dearly loved both animals. To further compound their problems, the German shepherd appeared to be going into a decline.

At about the same time, the husband acquired large quantities of mineral samples for re-sale, particularly focusing on quartz crystal and amethyst quartz. These were laid out on two tables in the living area for viewing by prospective clients and it soon became apparent that the Irish setter had developed a preference for the table on which the amethyst quartz was displayed and the German shepherd chose the table with the rock quartz on it.

Somewhat intrigued at their behaviour, my friends decided to try a simple experiment in order to ascertain that it was the minerals that drew the dogs to the different tables and not simply a preferred spot in the room. While the dogs were outdoors, the contents of the tables were exchanged, for they did not wish to forewarn them by simply moving the tables. They then sat down to await the return of both dogs.

Unerringly, the Irish setter made for the new location of the amethyst quartz, while the German shepherd made for the table upon which the quartz crystals now sat. From this experiment it would appear that each variety of quartz has an individual vibration, clearly recognisable by members of the Animal Kingdom.

My friends then decided to attempt a further experiment and tied a small bag containing a sample of their chosen mineral to the collar of each dog. The dogs responded very swiftly. The Irish setter, which now wore an amethyst crystal around its neck 24 hours a day, began to progress, the wound on its leg slowly beginning to heal, while the German shepherd acquired a great deal of energy, due no doubt to the close proximity of the clear quartz crystal, and in addition became relatively free of fleas.

Those of you who have pets with health problems may care to consider similar experiments, bearing in mind the fact that clear quartz crystal will stimulate activity, and milky or cloudy quartz will calm, making it ideal for over-active animals, while amethyst quartz purifies and heals, helping to deal with any number of afflictions.

19 Treating Plants

IF quartz crystals can produce positive benefits in both humans and animals, are they also able to assist plants? This and many similar questions are often asked, to which the short answer is 'yes'. In fact, some of the most startling occurrences take place once quartz crystals have been installed around plants.

I was recently the house guest of a close friend acting as temporary caretaker of a central city townhouse, the interior of which, although strikingly decorated, tended to be a little gloomy. In the midst of the gloom sat a very large tub filled with large, leafy plants, wilting due to over-watering. My host decided that the best treatment was a large dose of Canadian sunlight. Unfortunately for him, this rapid transition from gloom to bright sunlight only served to hasten the plants' demise, much to my host's chagrin.

At this point I decided to use a little crystal power, inserting a number of quartz crystals around the plants, leaving only their faceted tips peeping from the soil. Within a week the majority of the plants began to respond, sprouting much new growth, although the old leaves continued to yellow and wither. Only one plant refused to co-operate with the energy of the various quartz crystals, but the remainder continued their new growth, much to the relief of my host, who had not relished the prospect of telling their owner they had died.

This remarkable result was entirely due to the effect of the electromagnetic energies of the quartz crystals, which stimulated the chlorophyll within the structure of the plants, encouraging new growth. Indeed, all plant growth, whether it be in trees, shrubs or crops, is stimulated by the magnetic energies which permeate the Earth itself. Where there is prolific growth at any point, it is evidence of powerful magnetic forces in that region.

If your garden is not as productive as you would wish, make use of crystal power to stimulate growth. Square off the garden and select five medium-sized quartz crystals, burying four of them up to their faceted tips at each corner of that square. The fifth crystal should be set in the centre of the garden where it will draw the energies of all the other crystals inwards, leading in turn to vigorous growth throughout the garden.

However, should any plant or shrub within that square fail to respond to the influx of energy, take one of the crystals that has been sited at the corners of the square—not that which is centrally sited—and place it by the roots of the ailing plant. This will draw all of the energies of the other crystals and the combined force will stimulate growth.

One further experience I wish to share which clearly demonstrates the power crystals exercise over the Plant Kingdom. A woman was endeavouring to root some lemon grass so that it might be planted in her garden later, to provide a source of refreshing tea.

Placed in a pot of water on a sunny window ledge, it achieved little in the way of growth. I suggested that a quartz crystal placed several inches away from the pot might serve to stimulate growth. She did this, placing it well away from the window. The plant at this time was bent towards the light, seeking to absorb the life-giving rays of the Sun.

Within a matter of days the plant reversed its growth pattern, turning *away* from the Sun, seeking instead the stimulus of the quartz crystal. Even more important, it began to grow, much to the woman's delight.

Although sunlight is vital to all life forms, it would appear from this experience that the electromagnetic energies emanating from quartz crystals provide a more powerful form of attraction—at least in the Plant Kingdom.

20 Testing Bodily Defences

CHAKRA centres have their being in the 'outer' Etheric Body which completely surrounds the human form, where they form part of our front line of defence. It is essential to maintain these in a state of harmony at all times.

Of the many things that cause imbalance in the chakra system, the most important is negative or destructive thought patterns. But there are also a number of substances that are actually injurious to the physical body, some of which are willingly eaten or drunk or inhaled by large numbers of people everyday. Among these substances are tobacco, alcohol and narcotics.

Together with a willing volunteer (who must initially remain in ignorance of the nature of the substance to be so tested) a crystal therapist can publicly demonstrate the harmful nature of such preparations. This involves the use of a simple muscle-testing technique.

First, ask the volunteer to stretch out their right arm at shoulder height, advising them that you are about to attempt to push this down using only one finger. In the meantime they must use their muscle power to resist the attempt by pushing upwards.

The therapist may well discover that they have little success during this first attempt, for the volunteer, unless greatly depleted physically, will have no difficulty in resisting the pressure of your finger and will force their arm back to its original shoulder-high position. This first step serves to demonstrate to the volunteer and the public alike, the relative strength of their physical form.

Step two involves the therapist in a little devious deception. Ask a member of your audience to escort the volunteer from the room until both are well out of earshot, and then advise the audience of your intentions, assuring them that you will restore the individual concerned to full strength following the test.

Tobacco is a harmful substance and if introduced into the chakra system will immediately result in a marked drop in the level of physical strength. One unlit cigarette is sufficient to demonstrate this point, but the therapist must endeavor to keep it hidden from the volunteer.

Calling both individuals back into the room, request the volunteer to stand side-on to enable you to test a 'mystery' substance, assuring them that they will come to no harm. Place the cigarette 3 inches (8 cm) away from the Solar Plexus Chakra, leaving it there for some 3 or 4 minutes.

Pocketing the cigarette, request the volunteer to face the audience once more, raising their arm again to shoulder height. Pressing down with one finger the therapist should experience little difficulty in pushing the arm down to almost waist level, to the astonishment of the volunteer.

The therapist must now advise the individual concerned of the nature of the substance which has so alarmingly reduced their physical strength. Should the volunteer happen to be a heavy smoker this simple test is often sufficient to cause them to consider abandon-

ing the habit, together with many members of the audience.

This method can also be used to ascertain if an individual is in any way allergic to certain foods or compounds. Again, place a small sample of the substance concerned in close proximity to the solar plexus for several minutes, then test the arm muscles for any reaction. I know a number of people who use this method, particularly on small children, as it helps the child to come to understand their body's reaction to certain foods.

The therapist must, of course, seek to restore the physical strength of their somewhat rueful volunteer. Again, ask him or her to stand side-on, in order that the audience may clearly see what you now do. This time the therapist must introduce a clear quartz crystal into the region adjacent to the Solar Plexus Chakra,

focusing a thought pattern of 'light' through it for some 4–5 minutes.

Request the individual to face the audience once more, repeating again the muscle-testing technique using only one finger. Very little headway will be made, for the energy of the quartz crystal will have restored that individual's physical strength to its original level, leaving your volunteer able to resist any amount of pressure.

21   Better Exam Results

DUE to their uncanny ability to store memory patterns, quartz crystals can be utilised very effectively by all students, or indeed by anyone who must commit to memory a great deal of detailed information in a very short space of time.

Selecting two medium-sized crystals, one clear masculine, the other feminine, proceed to programme each in turn according to individual need. A simple programme such as 'record all mental patterns when instructed' would suffice, for the task ahead involves much mental activity. Provided that one repeats this instruction, coupled with a projection of 'love' towards the elemental intelligence of each crystal before each study session, placing the crystals on the work table before you, they will faithfully record all information which is fed into them. (One necessary warning: try to ensure that nobody else handles those crystals from that point on, for their thought patterns or emotions will clear the crystal memory bank.)

This astounding ability of quartz crystals has been proved on many occasions, but never so positively as with a close friend who recently commenced a 3-year course in naturopathy. This was to prove to be quite a challenge as her greatest disability was a perilously low vitality level which made long hours of detailed study extremely difficult. This weakness was compounded by surgery and, following a course of crystal therapy to restore her depleted vitality, I suggested that she use quartz crystals to assist her.

Approaching her first examination she became extremely apprehensive, but following my suggestions, she wore a yellow sweater (this being a colour which aids mental activity) and placed the masculine crystal on the floor between her feet, having first instructed the elemental intelligence to release all recorded information. As tension is a major factor in the failure rate among many students, she placed the feminine crystal on the desk beside her—again requesting that all recorded information be released. The masculine crystal between her feet released its activating force into her Etheric Form, providing her with mental and physical stimulus, while the gentler energy of the feminine crystal calmed her fears and doubts.

Free of stress and feeling calm, she duly completed all papers within the given time—and subsequently passed with a 95 per cent mark. Since that time, further examinations on subjects as taxing as anatomy and physiology have all been passed with equally high marks, all due—she is quite convinced—to the assistance given to her by the quartz crystals. There is, of course, no easy route to follow, for the student must play his or her part to the full and study attentively, in conjunction with duly programmed quartz crystals.

A humorous note. I would like to share an experience which took place during the course of a 7-day workshop recently. A 10-year-old young lady who was fascinated by quartz crystals was given permission to attend the first few days of the workshop accompanied by her mother. During this time she attentively listened to all I had to say and found that the quartz crystals she acquired did the most wondrous things. Unable to attend on the fourth day (she had to go to school) she solemnly handed her crystal to her mother asking her to take it to the workshop to record the information shared that day. Sadly, she was greatly disappointed, for her crystal, without her presence, was unable to achieve the desired result. If the relevant information has not also been recorded in our memory banks, a quartz crystal is unable to re-activate it.

Quartz cluster with both masculine and feminine energies.

22   The Hidden Powers of Gemstones

THE world upon which we currently have our being has in the past been termed 'the jewel in the firmament', and the views of the earth afforded us by spacecraft in recent years would certainly serve to confirm that point of view. However, deep beneath its surface, in what could perhaps be termed 'inner space', lie many rare and precious jewels which atom by atom are silently forming their light, awaiting discovery by mankind. When these are brought to the surface, cut and polished, we discover that they not only possess great beauty, but also powerful energies which may in turn be of great benefit to humanity.

Gemstones could be said to be concentrated points of light within the colour spectrum. Their healing qualities have long been known to mankind, and in the ancient civilisations their usage to eliminate physical disorders was developed into an exact science. With the dawning of modern Christianity this knowledge was suppressed because of the pagan significance the majority of such jewels bore; it is only in recent years that this knowledge has begun to re-surface.

All gemstones are created from the molten magma
which forms near the core of the planet and as this
restless mass erupts, flowing upwards towards the surface, it carries with it liquified minerals, gasses and
boiling geothermal waters which are deposited in the
many fissures that honeycomb the sub-strata.
Throughout the millions of years that comprise their
growth period, the embryo gems continually absorb
powerful electromagnetic energies which permeate
'inner space', and it is this force, coupled with their
mineral constituents, that so greatly benefit mankind.

Gemstones, not only quartz, can be used in several
beneficial ways, either worn upon the physical body,
where their in-built electromagnetic force will serve to
intensify the outer energy field which is termed the
Etheric Body, while stimulating the physical form in
the region where they are worn. Those who suffer
from disorders in the throat or from general weariness
due to worry or fear, should consider the benefits of
wearing a gem around the throat, particularly amber.

Where there is tension in the region of the solar
plexus due to increasing levels of sensitivity, a slice of
polished agate would certainly help to fend off negative or destructive vibrations. If under psychic attack,
a large piece of cornelian worn in the umbilical region
is said to be of great benefit.

One may also use gemstones to produce gem tinctures, a method used in the East, particularly India.
Here a gem is placed within a glass container of either
spring water or grain spirit, covered, and placed in
sunlight for a predetermined period, during which the
energies of the Sun will cause the liquid to absorb the
qualities of the gemstone. Today, other schools of
thought use variations of this method to produce colour tinctures and flower essences. It is certainly preferable to that which was followed by our forebears, who

tended to grind the jewels to powder and administer them internally, a somewhat dangerous practice, particularly when they contained poisonous substances, as malachite and other copper or lead-based minerals do.

One important factor when using gems as a healing therapy. To produce any worthwhile benefit the gemstones must be over 3 carats (600 mg) in weight. There are, of course, exceptions to every rule and where an individual has conscious knowledge of former life experiences wherein they used gemstones in a healing capacity, they are invariably able to produce many meaningful results with much smaller stones. But for most of us only 3-carat or heavier stones will do.

Rough, uncut stones often possess a far greater energy than those that have been cut and polished. Also these do not command the high prices of the latter. Select suitable uncut specimens and cleanse them by immersing them in sea salt and water for 24 hours to remove all residue, rinse under cold water and they are ready for use.

Throughout time the different gemstones have been linked to the various signs of the celestial zodiac, for certain gems do have positive benefits for individuals born under particular astrological signs. There is confusion about this subject; most adherents follow the lore of the jeweller. The information I share is that which accords with the teachings of ancient wisdom, and if one studies the general characteristics of those who are born under the different signs, and compare these with the qualities stimulated by the various gemstones, you will note that they correspond in a rather amazing manner.

Aries

The jewels linked to this, the first House in the Esoteric Zodiac, are the diamond, white sapphire and the
bloodstone, all of which help to overcome the many
nervous conditions caused by improper use of Martian
energies. Those born under this sign have the capacity
to become courageous pioneers, but do tend to rush in
where angels fear to tread, and all too often their suffering is caused by stubborn refusal to heed the advice
of others, and learn their lessons in life the difficult
way.

The diamond therefore signifies courage, stimulating this quality where it is lacking—as it so often is,
for many who incarnate under this sign tend to sink
into a state of apathy and despair when things do not
work out according to their grand plan. A diamond is
one of the hardest of stones, and the wearing of this
gem is intended to impart similar qualities of the average Arian subject. They were worn in the past by sol-
diery of different nations, usually upon their left arm
where the diamond facets caught the rays of the sun—
no doubt serving to distract the opposition in battle.
When diamonds are set around amethysts or emeralds
they serve to intensify the energy of those jewels, particularly with regard to the emerald, for when both
stones are focused along the spinal column of any individual they render particular benefits. In the past the
ancients utilised diamonds to create a sterile atmosphere or to purify a room.

The white sapphire (also known as the Asteria Sapphire) has an element of cloudiness in it, but also possesses 6 rays of light which appear at the upper part of
the stone. It is said to have the ability to bring peace to

a troubled mind—making it a positive stone for those who appear under the sign of Aries—this ability caused it to be termed the Star of Peace. The white sapphire is a secretive stone, much loved by those who are involved in occult practices, its qualities being recognised by eminent occultists throughout time. Pope Innocent III decreed that the Pope's ring should consist of a white star sapphire set in gold, largely because of the great peace these stones engender. Close affinity to a number of these stones worn in a form of talisman completely altered the personality of the Emperor Charlemagne.

The bloodstone is a form of green jasper containing a number of red marks, possibly formed by iron oxide. The Tibetans hung it around the neck of any individual who was prone to nose-bleed, or ground it up to place upon wounds, where it served to staunch the flow of blood.

Taurus

The stones which are linked to the sign of Taurus are the blue sapphire and the turquoise. These are stones which, when worn upon the person, will stimulate those energies which the average Taurean will require in order to overcome the problems they encounter in daily life.

The blue sapphire has long been regarded as *the* stone for those who desired spiritual enlightenment, for they help one to develop the powers of concentration. They are an initiate's stone and in the past were awarded as a mark of achievement to those who successfully sought to bring their wayward thought patterns under the control of the Higher Self. The blue sapphire is one of three gemstones that should not be purchased for personal use, particularly if one's thought patterns are erratic. If they are worn by intemperate Taureans they tend to lose their lustre.

The ancients used these stones for the treatment of all blood disorders, and in dealing with cases of smallpox they were placed on the eyes to prevent damage to the eyesight. Throughout time they have been used to treat all manner of eye problems, with positive results. In Tibet they were used for a different purpose. Due to their ability to bring about a measure of tranquility, they were placed by the Lamas in the hands of those departing the physical life to aid their transition to the Higher Planes.

The turquoise is generally known as the Stone of Venus, but many mistakenly allocate it to the sign of Capricorn.

The great quality of this gemstone lies in its ability to draw to itself any situation of conflict, its inner light acting as a barrier between its wearer and any negative thought patterns or harmful situations. For this reason the ancients termed it The Celestial Stone.

For those who suffer from grief, or shock arising from accidents, the Turquoise, when worn on the person, will bring about a measure of peace, for it is said to be a stone which possesses natural healing qualities, these being enhanced when the stone is set in silver.

Gemini

Allocated to the sign of Gemini are all varieties of agate and the chrysoprase.

The agate comes in many colours and is a variety of quartz, often located in fields where our forebears placed them to benefit nature. The moss agate is the most eagerly sought after for it contains in its construction all manner of natural substances which transform the stone into an art form. Possessing as they do a duality in their nature, the average Geminian gains a great deal from the wearing of an agate, for ancient wisdom indicates that agate has the potential to attract loyal friends, and have been worn for this specific purpose by many famous individuals, particularly Queen Elizabeth I of England. For anyone who is attempting to expand their spiritual horizons the agate is invaluable when worn over the solar plexus, for they help to deflect the often disturbing vibrations of others—often loved ones—whose innate fear of the unknown often leads to resentment of those who become embroiled in occult investigation.

The chrysoprase is, like the agate, a variety of quartz, tending to be apple-green in colour. It was believed by the ancients to help eliminate covetous thoughts and to stimulate the desire for success in new undertakings. It was therefore worn as an amulet by Alexander the Great, for whom it had great value. For anyone who desires to consciously activate their latent intuitive or clairvoyant faculties, the chrysoprase is a great asset and psychics have claimed that it has no equal in aiding sensitivity.

Agates and chrysoprase should *not* be worn by those born under the signs of Pisces or Virgo.

Cancer

There are five jewels allocated to the sign of Cancer: the emerald, moonstone, tiger's eye, pearls and quartz crystal.

Due to its healing properties, the most important stone linked to this sign is the emerald, utilised by all the ancient civilisations to cure eye disorders. The

Egyptians created large discs fashioned from gold, into which they affixed the relevant gemstone, through which the rays of the sun were then focused on the afflicted portion of the anatomy. When an emerald was so used, it brought swift relief from all bad eye conditions. In a less dramatic manner the Roman emperor, Nero, also capitalised on the energy of this gemstone. He suffered a great deal of pain in the region of the eyes and took to viewing the games through a very large emerald, for he discovered that it reduced the inflammation and took away the pain in his eyes. Those who are born under the sign of Cancer often have a poor memory and are also subject to giddiness; for such individuals, the emerald, set in a ring and worn constantly, will serve to protect them. The emerald is a very sensitive stone, whose energies serve to intensify the innate characteristics of those who wear them. Should one's astrological chart indicate the Moon to be in a bad aspect, it would be folly to wear an emerald, for its energies would merely serve to magnify those weaknesses which come under the influence of the Moon.

For most who appear under this astrological sign, the emerald is a wonderful stone for it aids the development of courage in these normally fearful individuals, and when used in healing will greatly relieve suffering located in the spinal region.

Moonstone is a variety of feldspar having a great affinity with the energies of the Moon, and, in common with the emerald, will assist in subduing fear in these very sensitive individuals. The Egyptians placed this in their great healing discs in order to treat asthma and lung disorders.

It is also possessed of properties that will aid those individuals who desire to develop their latent intuitive and clairvoyant faculties and is stated to particularly aid such activities when the Moon is on the wane.

The stone, tiger's eye, often referred to as 'imprisoned sunlight', is easily recognised by the golden stripe which runs through it. This is yet another stone which stimulates courage, particularly in children who are prone to nightmares. The Egyptians treated them with this stone set in great golden discs. It is stated that it has beneficial effects on those suffering from asthma, too.

Cancerians are credited with being possessive by nature, and in the tiger's eye they will discover a stone that will assist them to retain what they have acquired, and encourage thrift.

Many people have mixed feelings about pearls (not strictly a gemstone) due no doubt to their reputation for bringing bad luck or tears, which they may well do for any individual whose astrological chart reveals a poor aspect to the Moon. In the past the Chinese ground them up to enable the residue to be administered internally, for their mineral constituents were said to overcome giddiness and to aid intestinal disorders.

In ancient Egypt they developed a still-secret method of cauterising a wound with a ball of the purest quartz crystal. As spherical formations tend to disperse light in many directions it is assumed that the Egyptians devised a particular method of focusing a single beam of light through the ball which generated sufficient heat to seal the wound. Those born under the sign of Cancer tend to be extremely sensitive, and are easily affected by the waxing and waning of the Moon. Many possess latent mediumistic qualities which are also greatly influenced by the Moon. For those who desire to activate their 'inner' qualities, gazing into a

quartz crystal or crystal ball serves to stimulate the
Chakra centres which relate to these abilities.

Leo

Associated with the sign of Leo are the sardonyx,
chrysolite, tourmaline and amber. The main quality of
all of the Leo gems appears to be their ability to calm
fear of all kinds and when the lion roars it may be
because they fear something in their vicinity.

Sardonyx is a two-layered stone, the base being a
rich reddish-brown in colour with an upper layer of
white chalcedony. It was used to make cameos for it is
a very hard stone, and in common with agate it is believed to protect its wearer from infectious diseases,
giving off a vibration which could almost be termed
antiseptic in its action. Leos who have difficulty in retaining memory of everyday events should consider
wearing the stone to aid the retention of thought patterns; it is also said sardonyx will bring about a trans-
formation in a fractious personality, making the
individual more amenable to others.

Chrysolite is a very soft stone and comes in several
shades, ranging from bright green (when it is termed
peridot) to an olive shade (known as olivine). Its greatest virtue lies in its ability to still fear in its various
forms. The ancient name for this stone translates as
'precious gem' and in the past it was more eagerly
sought after than diamonds. Much favoured by the
Arabs, it was worn to help overcome fear of traversing
dark paths, and many Leos demonstrate a similar fear,
often avoiding such places. It is also stated that peridot
helps to calm fears stimulated by imagined heart irreg-
ularities—the heart being a weak point under the sign
of Leo. Following a great deal of nervous tension,

many a Leo imagines that they have developed a heart condition, undetectable to medical sources. The peridot will help to calm this fear and I can personally attest to this.

Tourmaline is a somewhat unusual stone due to its electrical properties, possessing both positive and negative poles. I would not personally recommend the wearing of either the black or green varieties on the person for any length of time for their potent energies can lead to over-stimulation of the bowels. There are many varieties of this gem, coming in pink, yellow, blue, white and red, plus a rare variety containing three quite separate colours within its make-up. When attracted to those around and about them, Leos tend to exude a great deal of vitality that can lead to a marked drop in their physical energies and the tourmaline, held in the hand for a short space of time, will swiftly restore this. Where such individuals are subject to fear or melancholy, the tourmaline will help them overcome such negative thoughts, and, it is said, will attract favours and friendship, the lack of which may well be the cause of the melancholy.

Amber is found in large quantities on the coast of the Baltic, particularly after a storm. It is actually not a stone at all but a fossil resin of an almost extinct species of pine and when discovered with the fossils of insects in it, attracts high prices. It is very soft and light, possessing electrical and magnetic properties, particularly when heated. It was often worn around the throat, where, due to the warmth it emits, was said to prevent the spread of infection, be of great benefit in treating colds, and its ability to cure throat and thyroid infections was said to be second to none. During the Roman Era it was worn to prevent or cure goitre. All yellow stones are said to have benefit for those born under the sign of Leo. Therefore the yellow beryl and the golden topaz can be worn to provide stimulus to all Leonine individuals.

Virgo

There are only two jewels allocated to the sign of Virgo, the cornelian and jade.

Cornelian appears in a number of shades, the red hue being the most highly prized by the ancients. It is a variety of chalcedony that is credited with the ability to calm anger, and when worn, to stimulate fluency of speech and the development of courage. It is also an invaluable aid to those who come under psychic attack. Sadly, this occurrence is not as infrequent as one might imagine and individuals who are determined to exert a measure of power over others utilise occult powers to achieve their goal. A large piece of cornelian, worn in the umbilical region (where the majority of such attacks are experienced) will help to ward off such forces. The ancients certainly understood this and a great deal of information on this subject is provided in the Egyptian Book of the Dead.

Jade was allocated to the sign of Virgo by the ancients for its ability to encourage purity of thought in its wearers and was termed 'the Jewel of the Gods' at one time. It is said to help prevent nightmares and to calm the fevers in a person that arise from kidney disorders. It comes in many shades, but only the green and lavender variety can safely be worn for any length of time.

Libra

The jewels allocated to the sign of Libra are the opal, coral and lapis lazuli.

Opal is a species of soft quartz and the wonderful play of colour is due to water that is trapped in its fissures. Opals can dry out and subsequently crack. When acquiring an opal one should ascertain just what effect they have on the solar plexus. Where they lead to an unpleasant churning in this region, then that particular gem is not for you. Opals are often considered to be unlucky and for those individuals who have the misfortune to have Venus badly aspected within their astrological chart, they may well prove to be so. Indeed, anyone who abuses the power of Venus (the planet of unconditional love) may soon discover the opal's ability to attract misfortune. In a similar manner, any Libran who consciously practices deceit will all too swiftly discover the negative vibration of an opal. In the past they were always used in the treatment of eye diseases, for the Latin name for this gem literally translates as 'eye-stone.' They are also credited with the ability to sharpen and strengthen the eyesight of those who wear them.

Although considered by many as a jewel, coral is actually a product of marine life and is not therefore a true gemstone. Its mineral constituents provide an indication of its true value to mankind, for it is composed of carbonate of lime, with small quantities of carbonate of magnesium and silica, plus magnesium fluoride and calcium. Indeed it was often ground up and administered internally to treat epilepsy in children, but was also stated by many authorities to strengthen the heart and the spleen; the latter being a weak spot in the physical make-up of those born under Libra.

Scorpio

Under the sign of Scorpio, the jewels allocated are the beryl, aquamarine, carbuncle and the lodestone.

The aquamarine and the beryl are very similar stones, differing only in colour. Aquamarine is a pale blue-green in its general appearance while beryl ranges from radiant blue to white. It is only in recent times that the aquamarine has become popular for the ancients preferred the beryl. The Egyptians used beryl in their healing discs to treat goitre and other infections of the thyroid gland, and its potent energies were said to transform those who demonstrated a predilection for idleness. Its major benefits lie in its abilities to stimulate visionary capacities. Most of those who are born under the sign of Scorpio are naturally psychic and given to the study of mystical subjects, and both the beryl and the aquamarine are utilised to activate latent visionary qualities in mankind. The ancients termed them 'the seer's stone'; ancient wisdom states that 'they enable seers to perceive visions'.

The carbuncle is basically a garnet, differing only in its outer appearance, for the carbuncle is usually a cabouchon or rounded stone, while the garnet is faceted. In common with most gemstones, there are masculine and feminine varieties, the former being deep red in colour, the latter much lighter red. The Egyptians used them in their great discs for cauterising wounds but the tribesmen of Northern India, lacking their skills, ground up the carbuncle, placing the residue on wounds that were sustained in battle. The powdered gem was also given internally to deal with acidity of the stomach and throat infections. They are said to have the capacity to enable a Scorpio to banish sadness, to bring peace to the mind when unjustly accused and to assist with the process of reconciliation.

The lodestone is a rather unusual form of mineral. Composed of oxides of iron, it does not have the appearance of a gemstone, for it is often covered in fragments of metallic substances and due to its magnetic properties is often termed 'magnetite'. It is a very potent mineral. Many Scorpio subjects prefer a high standard of living which in turn can lead to gout, a disorder that has its origin in the liver. When pieces of lodestone are affixed to the body in the region of that organ they are said to bring about a subtle healing energy, comforting to the individual concerned. When Scorpios are surrounded by opposition they tend to drain their outer energy fields, and the lodestone, held in the hand will help to restore this. The lodestone should never be worn by those who are born under the signs of Leo and Aquarius, who invariably have sufficient physical stimulus. Indeed, they should avoid all of the Scorpio gemstones, for their needs are of a different order.

Sagittarius

There are only two gemstones linked to this sign, the topaz and chrysolite.

Topaz comes in many colours but it is that variety that is almost orange in its hue that is the most effective for stimulating courage, joyfulness, or a feeling of contentment, that are the major virtues of this jewel. In Egypt it was known that the topaz would benefit those who suffered from asthma and it was utilised in one of two forms: either ground into powder and ap-

plied as a poultice to the upper portion of the body, or
placed in the golden healing discs. Topaz has a great
affinity with the Sun and the Egyptians utilised both to
treat this condition. Many Sagittarians suffer from in-
somnia—often linked to a disturbed mind and a faulty
circulation. Topaz, placed on the head in the region of
the temples is said to calm the mind, relax the body
and result in refreshing sleep. When dealing with those
who suffered the agonies of toothache, the Egyptians
powdered the topaz and administered this in wine,
with wonderful results—though which of the two was
the more successful is not stated!

Chrysolite and its two varieties, peridot and olivine,
have been discussed at length under the sign of Leo.

Capricorn

There are five gemstones linked to the sign of Capricorn: the ruby, spinel, malachite, onyx and jet.

The ruby is a greatly treasured gem, much sought
after throughout time. It is a perfect jewel for the
average Capricornian, for it brings about a measure of
peace in the midst of turmoil, aiding such individuals
to keep a tight rein on their emotions. A grim warning
for anyone intending to purchase a ruby. Should one's
astrological chart reveal opposition from Saturn it
would be folly to wear a ruby (or any of the jewels
allocated to the house of Capricorn) for they will
swiftly bring misfortune in their wake.

Capricorn is a sign linked to the element of Earth
and most who are influenced by it tend to set great
store by material possessions and where there is any
form of involvement in spiritual undertakings, it will
always be of a practical nature. Their choice of gemstones reflects this quality, and all jewels allocated to

this sign are more costly and heavier in appearance than most gemstones. In particular, those born under the signs of Aries and Libra should avoid these stones if Saturn is badly aspected in their astrological chart.

Spinel is also known as 'the Star Ruby' and is available in many colours, red, orange, green and violet. It has a gentle energy, devoid of the heavy vibrations attached to the ruby, and was particularly favoured in Chaldea and India. It was used as a protection against nightmare and to treat those who caught a chill or influenza. It was also said to energise the spleen, making it a very active yet sensitive stone.

Malachite contains a great deal of copper that provides its green hue, and great care should be exercised in using this stone for it is poisonous if taken internally. The ancients recommended it for use on children who suffered from colic, cramp and rheumatism (copper bracelets are still worn to this day to ward off this latter condition). Apparently this stone helps to tone up the muscles, preventing cramp, particularly in the intestines, and Capricornians are prone to such conditions.

Aquarius

Two gemstones are linked to the sign of Aquarius: jacinth and garnet.

Jacinth is a gemstone that bears many names but is possibly better known today as zircon, of which it is but one variety. Due to their flawless quality jacinth is often mistaken for diamond. However, lacking the carbon strength of the diamond, they tend to chip or crack, particularly along the facets. The ancients used these stones to calm fevers, especially those arising from a blood disorder.

Garnet was much revered by the ancients for its ability to forewarn of impending danger; it appears to lose all lustre when danger threatens. The mineral constituents of a garnet are said to be excellent for the treatment of all manner of blood disorders, to which many Aquarians are prone. Indeed most blood abnormalities that arise from long-term resentment manifest under this sign, and in the past the garnet was used in the treatment of fevers arising from such conditions.

Pisces

There is only one jewel linked to the sign of Pisces, the amethyst.

The amethyst is a somewhat unusual quartzstone, being the jewel that has long identified the Initiate and this gemstone, to be of esoteric value, must be freely bestowed by other individuals. An amethyst is possessed of a rare ability to bring about a return to harmony and balance in those upon whom its energies are focused, a vital quality for many born under the sign of Pisces, who can very often become unbalanced in their outlook due to emotional despair. Pisceans, in themselves are somewhat unusual in that the majority of their ailments arise due to their emotional response to everyday events, that only total rest and the mastery of their runaway emotions will cure. The energies of the amethyst will assist in this vital task. It also emits a purifying energy that directly influences the nervous system, although anyone who suffers from a severe personality disorder may find its vibrations uncongenial.

This information has been provided in answer to many requests for a general guide to the powers of certain gemstones, but it is only personal experience that will prove or disprove the theories of the ancient civilisations. One important point to bear in mind is that many of the gems sold today are synthetic and do not possess the vital electromagnetic energy of natural gemstones. Such stones will not therefore be capable of producing the desired results and should be avoided.

Tests conducted in our centre in the North of England have revealed that many individuals are able to gain great benefit from gemstones that do not correspond with their particular astrological sign, and the answer would appear to lie in whether or not the individual concerned responds to the vibration of a particular gemstone. Placing these in their hand prior to a therapeutic treatment, or while they relax following treatment has resulted in astonishing responses. Green dioptase, not classed as a gem, but whose beautiful rich emerald shade attracts many, emits a powerful energy that can be both stimulating and relaxing. Small hexagonal crystals of a mineral termed vanadenite have resulted in positive muscular responses in one individual who has long suffered from paralysis. Use of a golden beryl has resulted in lasting benefits in some who suffered from wasting diseases.

All form has life, all of which is linked to the Creative Force. Provided that one's motive is pure and that one bears in mind the necessity for the expression of unconditional love throughout such undertakings, all indicated substances can produce the desired result.

Bibliography

B. Bhattacharyya *Gem Therapies*

Ra Bonovitz *Cosmic Crystal*

H. L. Cayce *Edgar Cayce on Atlantis*

J. Lorusso & J. Glick *Healing Stoned*

John Michel *View Over Atlantis*

W. Richardson & L. Huett *Spiritual Value of Gem Stones*

Mona Rolfe *Initation by the Nile*

W. Scott-Elliott *The Lost Atlantis*

Da-El Walker *The Crystal Book*

American Yoga magazine

The Unexplained magazine

Acknowledgements

So many talented people have influenced my thinking during the past seven years, each in their own way acting as a teacher pointing out the path which lay ahead of me. Credit for initially opening my eyes to the powers of the mineral kingdom must go to Rita K.—my adversary Mnas Ra in *Vision Tomorrow*—whose channelling of information on how crystals were utilised in Atlantis sparked off my curiosity.

To Marcel Vogel I owe a great vote of thanks for an experience which made an indelible impression on my mind and subsequently upon my life. In a similar manner I am greatly indebted to Dr R. D. for the opportunity to work with crystals in his clinic, for that experience revealed new frontiers which even today I restlessly seek to extend. Also to Eliya my undying gratitude for acting as a spur, and for sharing the knowledge he had painstakingly gathered elsewhere. Indirectly, I am also indebted to the renowned crystal therapist and teacher, Da-el Walker, whose wisdom it was that Eliya shared with me in those early days, for this encouraged me to tap into my own subconscious storehouse.

I must also acknowledge two very special people who also served to fuel my enthusiasm, activating in the process, awareness of the powers of the Gem Kingdom—John R., whose knowledge of the power of light encouraged me to follow unknown paths; to him I will be eternally grateful for the introduction to the wondrous powers of gemstones. His late wife Nora was also a source of great inspiration, providing me— upon request from the Spirit Realm—with the information appertaining to the use of the various gemstones by the ancient races.

I have subsequently encountered many 'light bearers' on my travels, each in turn sharing a portion of the Ancient Wisdom, fuelling thereby the 'crystal fever' which is evident world-wide today. To the effervescent Soozi Holbeche, the practical Lyn Buess and the stimulating Harry Oldfield—my deep gratitude, for they have all played a part in the expansion of my consciousness.

To Ann Becker I am deeply grateful for her sketches of the chakra and endocrine systems.

David Charteris has again supported me with his photographs which involved much hard work in impossible surroundings, undertaken in love and with much humour.

About the Author

Spiritualist and world traveller, Edmund Harold is the president of the Sussex Spiritual Healing Organisation in the UK, and has long been the President of the Spiritual Venturers Association, which works in New Zealand, Australia, and the UK. He is the author of the bestselling VISION TOMORROW, HEALING FOR THE AQUARIAN AGE, and MASTER YOUR VIBRATION.